CW00419539

Understanding J. B. Pr Calls

- ## A Complete GCSE Study Guide for Summer 2015 & 2016 Exams.

By Gavin Smithers

Another one of **Gavin's Guides** – study books packed with insight. They aim to help you raise your grade!

Understanding J.B. Priestley's An Inspector Calls is a complete study guide and has been written especially for students and teachers who are preparing for GCSE in Summer 2015 and 2016.

Series Editor: Gill Chilton

Published by Gavin's Guides

Permission has been granted by United Artists on behalf of the Estate of the late J.B. Priestley to reproduce extracts from An Inspector Calls.

Let's Get Started

J.B. Priestley's "An Inspector Calls" has been a favourite GCSE text for many years. It's easy to see why; it asks questions about social equality and fairness, which are always relevant; it explores the age-old topic of who behaves and knows best, parents or children; it's quite short, with a small and easily understood number of characters; and it contains a unique surprise, at the very end of the play.

If you've bought this book because "An Inspector Calls" is included in what you have to study for GCSE, then, in my opinion, you've just taken another step towards doing well in your exam.

This guide has been written specifically to assist GCSE candidates who are taking the AQA, OCR and WJEC exams in 2015. It is also excellent to have on board early of course, if you are a current Year 10 student and whilst your GCSEs won't be until Summer 2016, you are studying this book in the first year of your course.

If you are entered for the AQA English Literature GCSE, you may like to know that just over 275,000 students took that exam in June 2014. Of these, 77% of candidates achieved a C grade or higher, but only 22% scored A or A*. Many would feel the real work to be done is in the weeks before you take your exam – transforming a general understanding and average way of putting your point across (that C grade) into one that will really make the examiner sit up and smile (that most pleasing A/A*).

During your exam, you will be expected to answer one question on the play, in approximately 40-45 minutes. It may well be about an individual character, or a key theme, or a critical moment or scene; but every question will allow you to show that you are familiar with the text, have something relevant and interesting to say, and can write an accurate and well organised essay.

In summer 2014, more than 126,000 students took their exams with WJEC. 73% achieved a grade C or better. 18% were awarded A or A*; 27% a B; and the next 28% a C. The exam which includes this play allows you an hour to answer a passage-based question (20 minutes) and also to choose from two questions as essay topics (40 minutes).

If your exam board is OCR, just over 31,000 candidates took the paper in 2014; 28% got an A or A*, and 80% achieved a C or higher. Under this exam board, you will have a choice of a passage-based question about one moment in the play, or a character-based essay. Each is worth 25% of your GCSE; the time allowed is currently 45 minutes in the exam.

"An Inspector Calls" raises big questions about our personal responsibility to others. There is also lively debate on the consequences of our actions. By getting to grips with these themes (and I show you how to do this) you'll be in line to impress the examiner.

But why a Gavin's Guide? It is likely you have browsed online or gone to a bookshop and discovered that there are a fair few study guides on this text already. Many of them are useful for summarising the plot and the characters.

<u>Few, if any, explain or analyse in as much detail as this guide does how Priestley manages and organises our response as we read.</u>

It is understanding this – and being able to communicate that you do to your examiner - that will mean you can achieve a good grade more easily.

I am a private tutor in Broadway, Worcestershire, and this book was initially written for my English Literature students. I wrote it to help them achieve good grades – and an understanding of what this principled, determined writer wanted to say. Now in e-book form or paperback, I hope it may help you too.

What this short guide can do

This guide can help you to understand clearly what Priestley wanted to say when he wrote "An Inspector Calls".

It will also help you to improve your essay technique.

And you will discover what examiners like, and don't like, to see in your answers.

If you find watching worthwhile as well as reading, then do try to find a production of the play at a theatre. In the past few years, productions have toured provincial towns and it is also a favourite with amateur dramatic companies. Do a google search with the play and your town to see if there is anything upcoming.

You can email me – at grnsmithers@hotmail.co.uk if you feel there is something that you still don't understand. I hope to help you further, or point you to further useful resources.

My love of literature began when I studied for an English degree at Oxford. Today, unravelling and appreciating language remains a lifelong passion. If this little book can move you towards that too – then it will be doubly worthwhile!

Interested? All you need is a few clear hours ... and a willingness to begin with an open, curious mind.

This short, interpretative guide is intended as a supplement to, not a substitute for, teaching in a school.

It also comes with a big warning

...this guide will tell you what happens in the play, almost from the start.

I make no apologies for 'plot spoiling' - as it is quite deliberate. A Study Guide is useful <u>after</u> you have read the play – it is not a 'short-cut' that means you don't have to!

At GCSE level, it is no longer enough to know what happened in a play. You need to look at the 'why' and 'how' of the way in which the writer has created his text.

Only by looking at the structure of each scene and seeing how it breaks down – sometimes as closely as word by word – can you gain full understanding.

Two ways to read the play

As you read this Gavin's Guide, do have your copy of the play to hand as well. Most schools provide non-marked copies especially for use during an exam. So if you want to use pencil, sticky notes or clips to help flag out particular sections – go right ahead!

Always remember that what you're reading … wasn't actually designed to be read! A play, unlike a book, has been written to be acted out. For an audience, a play is a drama that unfolds in front of them (us!) on stage. It is expressly designed to be enjoyed in one sitting.

As a student, you may have read the play, perhaps one act at a time, but still from beginning to end. Doing it this way of course replicates a little what you might experience were you watching the play – certainly you get a good sense of the pace and dramatic tension. It is also an easy way to see the key quotations and lines in their dramatic context. But there is a drawback! Doing it this way does not enable us to register how carefully Priestley has drawn the individual characters.

If you were acting in the play, you would concentrate first on your own part and learn your own lines.

So as a student who wants to go the extra mile to understand this clever play – this is what I suggest you do. No learning or stage skills are needed!

Rather, if you can get a second copy of the play, go through it with a packet of highlighter pens and mark the speeches of each character in a different colour.

Then, <u>look at each character in isolation</u>, as if you were preparing to play that part. You will notice that some characters (through their highlighter colours) are absent from time to time, and <u>that each of them undergoes their own "inspection"</u>.

When you become aware of the grinding, remorseless methods the inspector uses, you will feel some empathy for the nervousness Sheila, Gerald and Eric experience, and you will feel frustrated at the stupidity and self-satisfaction of Arthur and Sybil Birling. You will also, I believe, be close to understanding the play's full power. More of that later! For now, let's start with the playwright himself...

The life and times of J. B. Priestley

John Boynton Priestley was born on 13 September 1894, and died on 14 August 1984, aged 89.He went to a grammar school in Bradford, and then worked as a clerk. He was old enough to fight in the First World War, volunteering at the age of 18. He was wounded, and also injured in a gas attack and then judged unfit for active service.

He went to Cambridge University, to complete a degree in Modern History and Political Science. In 1921, he moved to London, and began to work as a freelance writer. He wrote 16 novels and about 50 plays, as well as journalism, broadcasting and literary criticism. He had a long career as a political and social commentator. He co- founded the socialist Common Wealth Party in 1941, was a strong supporter of the Campaign for Nuclear Disarmament and was a British delegate to UNESCO.

Priestley refused both a knighthood and a peerage, but accepted membership of the Order of Merit, because it was unconnected with political activity.

In the context of his interests and beliefs, we can understand why Priestley chose to set "An Inspector Calls" in the year 1912, even though it was only seen by audiences from 1946 onwards. The central premise of the play is that the strong and powerful in society need to take responsibility for the weak and powerless- particularly unskilled workers who have no economic power.

The years before the outbreak of the First World War in 1914 were a time of industrial and social unrest. Britain had a population of 33 million, but 10 million people were living in poverty. In 1906, jobless people from the Midlands marched to London to protest about their lack of opportunity. Cotton workers went on strike in 1908, and there was a miners' strike in 1910- a year in which 700 cotton mills in Lancashire locked out workers who were demanding higher wages. This is precisely the issue Priestley uses to motivate the start of Eva Smith's tragedy. 1912 saw further protests by workers in clothing factories, and riots caused by the acute poverty of the poorest-paid.

In 1909, the Liberal Government raised taxes in a "People's Budget", to try to accelerate social reform. National Insurance and unemployment benefits were introduced for the first time in 1911 and medical welfare for the poor extended the range of the benefits system. Sickness and maternity benefits followed, in 1913, a year in which 400 miners died in a pit fire. In 1914, 140000 miners and 20000 builders went on strike. The costs of the War led to a doubling of income tax.

The historical facts show us how wrong Mr Birling is, on almost everything he has an opinion about. Even in his own time, he is a backward-looking and unenlightened employer, resisting the curve of social progress, and blind to the problems in the community just outside his own front door. He is sitting in his comfortable house telling anyone who will listen that all's well in the world, and he is so out of touch that the Inspector has to pay him a visit (or two) in order to show him what it is like to live in the real world.

Priestley himself wrote a very sane and interesting book, "The Edwardians", when he was 75; it was published in 1970. He analyses the culture of the era he grew up in- the era in which he sets this play- as one where the rich were too rich and the poor too poor, but where there was no appetite for violent or revolutionary political action. The last twenty years of the Victorian era had been a time of falling living standards and growing insecurity, except for people who were already rich (like the Croft family) or people who had gained more recently from "cheap labour" and a growth in economic markets (the Birlings).

The expansion of international shipping, in which Britain was a word leader, promoted global trade, but it also opened its home market up to cheaper competition from abroad. British farmers, manufacturers, mine owners and industrialists tended to resist adopting new and more efficient work practices. The old-fashioned complacency of Arthur Birling reflects the loss of a competitive edge (to the USA in particular) which the domestic economy was beginning to experience.

The inequality of wealth and security is at the heart of the play, because the Birlings have built their own prosperity on the bedrock of refusing to pay more for "cheap labour". All industrialised countries were in a race to develop the range and size of their exports; to protect their domestic markets from cheap imports; and to be "smart".

These economic challenges could only be conquered if men like Birling saw the bigger picture and behaved in a responsible and enlightened way; Arthur Birling is too narrow-minded, too "provincial", to do that. The Inspector tells him he has a public responsibility (to promote the welfare of his employees and community, as well as his own family); Birling rejects this as "nonsense", which leaves the lesson of the tragedy of Eva Smith unlearnt, and bound to be repeated.

It is certainly uncomfortable that a man like Birling can be a former Lord Mayor, councillor and magistrate and be touched so little by what he sees. He may be said to give the word "selfish" new meaning!!

Certainly, Britain had its social problems in the decade prior to the First World War. Working-class poverty and rising commodity prices squeezed standards of living for those who were less well off, but the middle classes- from which Priestley himself came- worried that higher wages for semi-skilled workers (which had already driven people out of the countryside and into the towns) would lead to social instability.

It seems odd to us now, but when the House of Lords blocked many of the (Liberal) government's attempts to address some of the most obvious inequalities, two snap elections in 1910 failed to secure a public mandate for the changes which were clearly needed. It wasn't that people didn't hate being poor – of course they did! Rather it was that change (even good change) seemed too radical and different to be possible.

The idea that it was the business of a government to tax its citizens and spend their money centrally had not yet taken root. Because we live in a world long accustomed to the huge extension of the welfare state, our outlook tends to be very different- although the question of how much any government should tax and spend is asked in every decade.

Priestley sees Edwardian society as anxious, deferential and traditional; fearful of change, and optimistic; over-confident (he writes in his own history of the period, at length, about the social significance of the sinking of the Titanic in 1912) and yet tolerant of radical thought; sexually conservative, but relaxed about personal morality.

Priestley himself saw the election of Attlee's Labour government in 1945 as the key to dismantling the British Empire peacefully (a necessary step), and he traces that election result back to the years between 1906 and 1912- the year in which he sets "An Inspector Calls". The liberal thinking of the time may have been slow to address the inequalities of the old class system, and it may have lacked intelligence and bite, but Priestley sees more good than bad in a period where the welfare system put down its first real roots, so that the idea of social conscience could begin to take hold.

What he is saying in the play is that those foundations now have to be built upon, and that Governments must reflect the new social conscience which ordinary citizens have developed since the time of Arthur and Sybil Birling.

Priestley's own analysis of the Edwardian era, as a historian, is interesting because it shows us his breadth of interests, and the generosity of his judgments. Its relevance to "An Inspector Calls" is that the play's representation of the three classes- lower (Eva Smith), middle (the Birlings) and upper (the Crofts)- encapsulates and defines the social problem, both of 1912, but more particularly of 1945 onwards – which is what his audience (watching the play in the late 1940s) would be interested in too.

Priestley is not a "crank", in the sense of wanting a revolution to sweep away the old order (despite the Inspector's violent language, and his impatience). Priestley sees the post-War era as a defining moment, in which there is a unique opportunity- and responsibility- to address the question "what sort of society, or community, do we want to construct?"

As a dramatist, Priestley uses his power as a playwright to do two things:

Firstly, to entertain and engage the audience, by letting the drama unfold in a suspenseful way, and with a surprise right at the end of the play; and, **secondly**, to give the evening in the theatre a moral resonance which goes beyond what merely entertains us.

Serious drama seeks to "teach" us something about our responsibilities as citizens.

We may feel, seventy years later, that Priestley goes too far in "preaching" his social message. The Inspector works better as a dramatic device than as a character; he is rather robotic and repetitive. It is fair to say that, for example, Arthur Miller's "The Crucible" (1953) is a much subtler representation of the weaknesses of the society the playwright wants to dissect. However, no audience will fail to appreciate the dramatic skill which underpins and organises Priestley's plot.

"An Inspector Calls" is, then, a very distinctive play, first performed in 1946, but set in the spring of 1912. That period of 34 years is less than half a lifetime, but it spans two World Wars, the Great Depression, the Russian Revolution and the rise of communism and fascism, and the development of labour-saving mass production.

The costumes, stage furniture and language of the play may seem authentic for 1912, but why did Priestley choose that particular, and precise, year?

The answer is that it enables him to contrast the "old world" of the Edwardians, which, he feels, sleepwalked into war and upheaval, with the world of the audience for whom he has written the play. If those who have survived a Second World War do not learn its lessons, will there have to be a third World War in another few years' time?

Priestley does not put his analysis of the ills and dangers to society directly into the mouths of his characters. It is through their personalities and their behaviour- selfish, complacent, careless, self-obsessed- that he advances his belief that a cohesive society is one in which wealth and comfort are shared, and there is a sense of community; in particular, the disadvantaged must be treated with respect and dignity, and be given opportunities to improve the quality of their lives. It is unforgivable to exploit the weak.

The alternative is a world where workers have to take by force what they should be entitled to by right. Unchecked, oppression- by employers like the Croft family and Arthur Birling- will make revolution inevitable. Writers who had grown up with the 20th century, and seen the emergence of communism, the growth in industrial mass production, and the entrenched ideology of capitalism, were interested in how these tensions can be resolved.

In America, John Steinbeck (1902-1968) arrived at much the same conclusion as (the slightly older) Priestley, in his great novel of 1939, "The Grapes of Wrath"- that inequality of incomes threatens social stability- although Steinbeck is less interested in advocating the British model of the welfare state.

By making the elder Birlings selfish and backward-looking, Priestley aligns capitalism with a regressive view of the world. They are wealthy, complacent, and always wrong, because they are small-minded and selfish. In the most famous speech in the play (in Act 3), the Inspector warns Arthur Birling of the social upheaval which will follow unless people like him now develop a proper sense of responsibility and care towards people beyond their immediate family.

Priestley's achievement is to dramatise the clash of the ideologies of the Left and the Right, with the Inspector advocating social responsibility and a new morality- he is a socialist. The Birlings are capitalists, who rely on the class system to maintain their power and excuse their shabby morality, hypocrisy and grubby secrets.

Subsequent history suggests that Priestley over-dramatised the problem of social cohesion; we haven't had a revolution, and communism has failed, while free-market economies have succeeded.

But, even if we find Priestley's own values and beliefs overstated in the play, and his analysis of what makes a better society oversimplified, we can still admire his skill as a dramatist. The issues he raises were at the forefront of the minds of those who had emerged from the Second World War hoping for a peaceful and harmonious future.

Summarizing and understanding the Plot

The action of the play takes place over a single evening. Mr and Mrs Birling and their son Eric are celebrating the engagement of their daughter Sheila to Gerald Croft, the son of Sir George and Lady Croft, an aristocratic family who own the manufacturing business which competes with theirs.

For Mr Birling, the forthcoming marriage (or merger) will cement their separation from the lower-class world from where they take their employees ("cheap labour"). He hopes that the knighthood he is expecting will make his family acceptable to the Crofts.

As Mr Birling sets out his (wholly mistaken) opinions about how the world will look over the next thirty years, the gathering is rudely interrupted. An "Inspector" has arrived to ask some questions about a girl who has committed suicide by swallowing a toxic disinfectant.

The Inspector implicates each member of the family, and their prospective son-in-law, in the process which led to the suicide, one at a time- first Mr Birling, then Sheila, then Gerald, then Mrs Birling, then Eric. His revelations make them all face uncomfortable truths about themselves and each other. The engagement is called off, and the Inspector leaves them "to adjust their relationships".

Mrs Birling appears to be responsible for the death of her son's unborn child, because she has refused charitable help to the desperately needy girl whose pregnancy has come about from her unfortunate and reluctant relationship with Mrs Birling's own drunken child.

The characters sense, afterwards, that the Inspector knew too much, and behaved eccentrically. Gerald and Mr Birling establish that the Inspector is not a member of the local police force, and that there has been no death by suicide reported to the local hospital.

They react to those facts by excusing themselves for their bad behaviour, because it seems that the actions the Inspector has criticised them for have had no consequences in the real world; there will be no public scandal, and Mr Birling will get his knighthood after all. But the younger Birlings- Eric and Sheila- now realise that immoral behaviour is what it is, regardless of whether there is a public revelation of it. Crimes of conscience are still crimes, whether they are publicly exposed or not. Sheila, therefore, cannot ignore Gerald's deceptions and lies, and marry him regardless; the inspection they have been through has left them different people from who and what they were at the start of the evening.

Because the older generation, and Gerald, regard the whole episode as a joke, or a lucky escape, they think they can ignore the lessons which they need to learn about personal morality and their social responsibility. Therefore the play ends with a dramatically stunning coup- the phone rings and Mr Birling is told that a girl has now died in the way the Inspector had described; and an Inspector is on the way, to question the family.

Whatever the "truth" is – whether there is a real death or not- the characters cannot, and should not try to, avoid taking responsibility for their own behaviour. The audience leaves the theatre wondering whether the characters will be humbler, and more receptive, the second time around, to the Inspector's demands that they face their own selfishness and mistakes honestly, and change their way of living.

Detailed Commentary

Act One

The play begins with some unusually detailed stage directions, in which Priestley acknowledges that it is possible to stage the play either with "a realistic set", or, presumably, with one less "ordinary". This immediately raises the question of how important it is to anchor the play in its setting of 1912. What matters most is not the props on the stage but how to dramatize the stripping away of the Birlings' dishonesty and complacency.

Because it is a morality play, realism matters less than meaning.

These stage directions emphasize two things- heaviness and coldness. The Birlings' house is like a furnished bunker- "heavily comfortable, but not cosy and homelike"; Mr Birling is "heavy-looking" and Mrs Birling is "a rather cold woman".

The absence of warmth is figurative as well as literal. The Birling parents are coldly superior because they think they are entitled to be so. The events of the play will show that their façade of superiority masks their criminal inhumanity only thinly; the Inspector soon dismantles the veneer of solid respectability.

They are finishing a celebratory meal. Priestley says that there is no tablecloth; not having one means not having to wash and iron one. Is this in itself a sign of the Birlings' essential meanness of spirit? Or would a table cloth be uncomfortably like a shroud for Eva Smith?

The diners are "pleased with themselves" and Sheila is "very pleased with life and rather excited" because this is the evening of her engagement to Gerald. Eric, by contrast, is "not quite at ease", because he knows about Gerald's disloyalty to Sheila and his complacent lying about it. He also has a guilty secret of his own- the fact that he is to be the father of an illegitimate child.

Mr Birling opens the play with the observation that the port they are drinking is the same brand Gerald's father buys. Mr Birling is aping the style of the aristocracy, and aspiring to be accepted by his social superiors; but it is precisely this breaking down of social barriers to aspiration which he resisted when he sacked Eva. His vulgarity and social maladroitness are apparent again, when he tells his wife to congratulate "cook from me" on the "good dinner", he commits a faux pas in front of Gerald, their more aristocratic guest. In those days, someone of high breeding would never mention that they had servants (who would serve as if invisible), let alone send praise to them.

Sheila's disparaging comment about "purple-faced old men" creates an immediate tension between the younger generation and the parents.

Mrs Birling is a reluctant drinker, unlike the men, who lubricate their conversation plentifully (they have had champagne with the meal, port now, with large amounts of whisky to follow). She makes excuses for the way Sheila says Gerald had neglected her "all last summer", on the grounds that

"men with important work to do sometimes have to spend nearly all their time and energy on their business".

This is ironic, as Gerald was in fact spending all his time and energy on Eva Smith, a prettier and more submissive version of Sheila. Sheila's warning to Gerald, to "be careful", has layers of ironic meaning. Gerald has been careful to conceal his relationship with Eva and to deceive Sheila over it; he was careful not to make her pregnant; and Eric's sudden "guffaw", or unexplained and inappropriate laughter, means that he himself was not so careful. Eva is his guilty secret, as well as Gerald's.

The older Birlings- both Arthur and Sybil- turn a blind eye to male indiscretion. It is difficult to believe that they have seen no signs that Eric is an alcoholic- they simply choose to ignore what is awkward or messy or difficult to deal with. Sheila accuses Eric of being "squiffy", or drunk; her mother moves the talk on, so that Mr Birling can overlook Eric's request that he doesn't make a speech.

Mr Birling is less interested in the "happy" couple than in the prospect of the two family businesses "working together – for lower costs and higher prices".

Crofts is "older and bigger" than Birling and Co. Arthur Birling is always looking for opportunities to consolidate or improve his social and financial security. As a self-made man, he is insecure about his position, and so he is selfish and insular, when, in Priestley's view, he should be willing to share some of his profits by paying his employees more. Mr Birling is too stupid to see that the inferiority he feels towards the Croft family is a mirror image of the insecurity the "Eva Smiths and John Smiths" suffer because they are treated merely as cheap labour. His own aspiration- to make more money, through higher profit margins, and thus become more secure- is one he does not permit his employees to share.

Gerald refers to himself now as fortunate "this once anyhow"- an oblique reference to his bad decision, in deceiving Sheila; and Eric refers to Sheila's "nasty temper sometimes", which is her key fault, and the source of her guilt.

After Gerald has given Sheila the engagement ring, which, she says, she will never let out of her sight (ironically, because she gives it back to him half way through Act Two), Mr Birling launches into his complacent view of the world.

In his judgment, "this is a very good time" because "we employers are at last coming together" to protect capitalism against strikes and social unrest. The strength of capitalists will lead to "a time of steadily increasing prosperity"; there will be no war, because "The Germans don't want war"; the Titanic is "unsinkable, absolutely unsinkable". He predicts that, in 1940, opposition to capitalism will be a thing of the past, and there will be peace and prosperity and progress everywhere, except in Russia (the home of communism).

History, of course, discredits Arthur Birling completely, with devastating dramatic irony. The Titanic sank on its maiden voyage. The Germans initiated both World Wars. And in 1940 the threat of an invasion of Britain was very real indeed.

He insists that, as a "hard-headed business man", he understands the wider world, through his knowledge and experience. This is fatuous, because he is so limited in his vision. He sneers at reformist social thinkers like Bernard Shaw and HG Wells. Then, once again, as soon as the women have left the room, he tries to ingratiate himself with

Gerald, by confiding in him that he expects to be given a knighthood, "so long as we behave ourselves, don't get into the police court or start a scandal".

The irony is that he is already caught up in such a scandal, without realising it. He may have been Lord Mayor, and may be "regarded as a sound useful party man" but he is a bad employer, a bad parent, and a mediocre human being.

Note the stage direction here- he "laughs complacently". His self-satisfaction deserves to be dismantled. There is hidden irony in Gerald's observation "you seem to be a nice well-behaved family" and Birling's agreement that "we think we are"; the play will strip away the complacency and the appearance of respectability, to revel the immorality they are pretending they are not guilty of. The upper and middle classes are fools who fool themselves.

When Eric comes back into the room in search of "another glass of port" he almost starts telling the "story" of his involvement with Eva. When he stops himself, his father refers to the fact that, with "more money to spend and more time to spare" than his own generation, men of Eric's age will be freer and so able to have more fun than his own age group had, when they were young. Mr Birling senior isn't saying that this is a problem, but just that this is how things are.

However, we will soon know that what Eric has been doing with his father's money and his spare time – making Eva pregnant- will emerge in Act Three. The dissolute way of life his parents allow Eric to pursue is precisely the wrong one for him.

More "solemnly" Birling also tells Gerald and Eric that a man's responsibility is to "look after himself- and his family" and "mind his own business". He says this in order to reject the idea of "community and all that nonsense". He believes that, while we are responsible for our immediate family, we have no duty to look beyond that. He has learnt that, he insists, from "the good hard school of experience".

But the Inspector will show us that Mr Birling has learnt nothing about social responsibility, and has not even managed his own "business" well- he has turned a blind eye to all the people and issues he should have taken responsibility for, including his son and the people he employs.

The Inspector arrives while Arthur Birling is in mid-sentence, on the subject of his doctrine of individualism. Before he is shown in, Gerald laughs off the visit, saying that the police are unnecessary "unless Eric's been up to something" (which, of course, he has).

Eric is "uneasy", and there is an instant where his father may detect the possibility that he is hiding something, but the Inspector's entrance cuts off the chance to explore that.

"Inspector Goole" is about the same age as Arthur Birling; he looks at whomever he is talking to in a penetrating way, and conveys "an impression of massiveness, solidity and purposefulness". He is a serious character, without any of the pretensions of the Birling family. Offered the inevitable drink, he points out to Mr Birling that "I'm on duty". The audience will pick up the inference that no-one else is doing their duty in a moral, rather than police sense of the word!

The Inspector claims that he "was recently transferred", which is why Mr Birling has not met him or heard of him before. He announces that he is seeking "information" about the "suicide" "two hours ago" of "a young woman" who had "swallowed a lot of strong disinfectant" "this afternoon".

Mr Birling, who embodies the concept that an Englishman's home is his castle, is dismissive. The Inspector asks him if he remembers Eva Smith, and he shows him a photograph. Gerald and Eric want to see it, too, but the Inspector prevents them, saying that he likes "to work...one person...at a time."

This is vital to the plot; Priestley wants to uncover each character's guilt in a linear or serial way. There would be a fatal loss of dramatic tension, and focus, if any of the characters understood more than they do, out of their turn.

Birling remembers that he "discharged" or dismissed Eva, almost two years previously, in the autumn of 1910. Gerald tries to excuse himself from the discussion, but, once the Inspector knows that he and Sheila are engaged, he says that he requires him ("gravely") to stay.

Mr Birling offers the- apparently reasonable- opinion that so much time had passed between her sacking and her death that the two events cannot possibly be connected. The Inspector contradicts him, saying that "what happened to her then may have determined what happened to her afterwards…driven her to suicide…a chain of events".

The Inspector is challenging Mr Birling's inability to see that actions have consequences- even if they are delayed or unintended. We squirm a little when Birling insists "I can't accept any responsibility", because "it would be very awkward" to be responsible for people outside our sphere of responsibility. He now wants to suppress what Eric reminds him he has just said, to the effect that "a man has to look after himself" (and not other people).

Arthur Birling has complete recall of the details of the pay dispute. Eva had been "a good worker" who was about to be promoted (and paid more)-but Mr Birling is the sort of man who will always round costs up and profits down, and then seek to make more profit while reducing costs (including wage rates) whenever he can. He evaluates the strike in terms of the extra wages he was asked for, and he says it would have "added about twelve per cent" to the labour costs (technically, it is nearer to 11%).

His argument is that the market dictates the going rate for the job; he pays no less or more than his competitors. From his point of view, breaking ranks and offering a rogue pay rise would start a costs war and erode profits in his industry. From the point of view of his employees, this is a wage-fixing cartel; they could not negotiate, so they went on strike, briefly, but the strike was a "pitiful affair" which petered out "after a week or two" because the strikers could not afford to be out of work. Birling reinstated them all, at the old pay rates, except for the "four or five ring-leaders", which included Eva. She "had to go", he makes clear, because she spoke out and "she'd had a lot to say – far too much".

This detailed account of the strike dramatizes the imbalance of power between the (authoritarian) employer, the owner of the means of production, and the powerless (and only politely revolutionary) workers, who only have their own labour to bargain with- labour being a cheap commodity which the employer can find easily elsewhere.

Gerald condones Birling's decision to "come down sharply" on the ringleaders, to discourage the rest (as if he is running a conscript army, not a family firm). Eric says that his father should have kept Eva in her job. The Inspector is on the side of the powerless and says "it's better to ask for the earth than to take it."

The idea that revolution is the only really effective form of protest left would become a historical fact, soon enough, in Russia in 1917; Birling has already described Russia as a country "which will always be behindhand naturally". He cannot see that his own hard-line capitalism is not sustainable, without (as Priestley sees it, also) being morally offensive, negligent, and the cause of justifiable social unrest.

He does not allow Eric's view any consideration, ("just you keep out of this… rubbish"). He has failed to take an interest in how Eric lives his life (with disastrous consequences, as we find out later), and his style of behaving to his son- arrogant, authoritarian, and dismissive- indicates that his faults run deep.

He has provided Eric with an expensive public school and university education but is incapable of being an effective parent. Eric points out that asking for higher pay is no different from charging higher prices; Birling loses his temper, and tells him (ironically) "it's about time you learnt to face a few responsibilities". While that is true of Eric's personal behaviour, he has surely picked up his irresponsible attitude (or belief that he has no responsibility to or for other people) from his own father.

Birling makes a clumsy threat to the Inspector about his golfing friendship with the Chief Constable, and threatens to "report" him for being "officious". This makes no impression on the "Inspector", because, as we will realise later, he is not part of the official police force. He naturally assumes that Eva's path was a downward one; he asks the Inspector whether she got "into trouble", or went "on the streets" (became a prostitute). The Inspector's reply- "no she didn't exactly go on the streets"- seems harmless, but we will see that Gerald and Eric have, in their turn, virtually reduced her to that exploited and worthless position- a prostitute.

The Inspector refuses to be rushed here; later in the play, as the dramatic tension rises, he says he has little time, because Priestley then wants to move the plot along more quickly. Sheila's appearance prompts the Inspector to present himself to her as "a police inspector", and to tell her that the dead girl was 24, and had been very pretty. This establishes a link between Sheila and Eva- they are more similar than the gulf in their social positions implies.

He challenges Gerald's assertion that "we don't know" what happened to Eva after she was sacked from Birling's. Now, the three Birlings present, and Gerald, "exchange bewildered and perturbed glances", their bubble of complacency and insularity seems less solid.

It is Sheila's turn to mention the "R" word – "you talk as if we were responsible" - and Birling's response to the accusation of guilt aimed at his daughter is to "talk this over quietly in a corner… settle it sensibly for you" or try to secure the Inspector's silence somehow (to avoid the scandal which might deprive him of his knighthood and his respectability). He thinks that bribery is a legitimate use of the power of money, and intimidation a legitimate use of social connections.

Gerald says- truthfully but mistakenly- that he has "never known an Eva Smith", and Sheila says that she has "never heard it before" either. The Inspector reveals that she changed her name. As he had done with Eric, Birling refutes Sheila's view that sacking her was mean, describing such a criticism as "rubbish".

The Inspector reveals a little about Eva's precarious life after losing her job in September 1910. She had no job at all for two months; no parents to help her; no savings, few friends, and little food. He universalises her predicament, saying that it is not an isolated case- the factories and warehouses, which take advantage of "cheap labour", condemn young women in every town and city to "that sort of existence". Sheila objects to the term "cheap labour"- "they're people" not a cliche- and the Inspector agrees with her that it is correct to empathise with these victims of economic exploitation.

But he resumes his relentless grind to reveal guilt. Eva thought her job at Milwards in December 2010 was "a wonderful stroke of luck", and "a good fresh start". When he says she lost that job, Mr Birling assumes it is for poor performance; but it was because "a customer complained about her" at the end of January 1911. Sheila recognises immediately that she was the customer; confirms the identity of the shop assistant by looking at the Inspector's photograph of her; and runs out, distressed.

Mr Birling accuses the Inspector of making "a nasty mess" of a "nice little family celebration", and says he must tell his wife what is going on. The Inspector turns Birling's words against him, sarcastically- somebody has made "a nasty mess" of Eva's "nice little promising life". We would not expect a real policeman to speak like this, but Birling leaves the room, without challenging him.

This leaves Gerald and Eric, both of whom are "uneasy", with the Inspector. Gerald asks to see the photo, but the Inspector refuses, again. This is because Priestley wants to handle the events of Eva's decline, and the guilt which goes with it, in chronological order; Mr Birling's sacking of her, Sheila's malevolence, then, "soon"- but only, for dramatic impact, when Sheila has come back- Gerald's use of her as a mistress. Eric tries to excuse himself, on the grounds that he has an alcohol-induced headache, but the Inspector tells him to stay.

Gerald objects to the Inspector's manner, saying "we're respectable citizens and not criminals". The Inspector says that the line between the two is not so clear; that is, there are crimes which are against the law, and there are crimes against conscience. We will return elsewhere in this guide to the concept of the seven deadly sins; actions and attitudes may still be wrong, in the sense of being "sins" or moral offences, even when they are not criminal offences. Gerald is relieved that "crime" is not defined in the Inspector's moral terms; the Inspector states that "inquiries of this sort"- into the consciences and morality of the complacent property-owning classes- "are left to me".

Sheila returns, to admit her guilt, and be told that Eva's next decision was to "try another kind of life"- being a kept woman, or quasi-prostitute. The Inspector judges that Sheila is partly, not entirely, responsible, for Eva's suicide; as her father is.

Like her father, Sheila had used her economic power to deprive Eva of her job- she had threatened to close the family's account otherwise, simply because of the "furious temper" she was in. In fact, she was already in a bad temper and then became angrier still as she realised that the dress she was trying on would look dreadful on her, but great on Eva.

With the self-knowledge and honesty which is beyond Arthur Birling, Sheila confesses that she was motivated by spite- if Eva had been plain instead of pretty, she would not have been malicious, but she thought that a girl like Eva "could take care of herself". The Inspector judges that Sheila "used the power you had" to "punish" her because she was "jealous" of Eva's aptitude for wearing that particular dress.

Sheila says that this is the only time she has behaved like that, and that she will never do so again. Her acknowledgment of her "crime", and her penitence, contrast sharply with her father's self-justification and denial.

The Inspector mentions that Eva adopted a new name- Daisy Renton-which startles Gerald. Sheila sends Eric and the Inspector out, and confronts her fiancé with his disloyalty and deception. Sheila's intuition for uncovering Gerald's secret is as powerful as the Inspector's.

Confronted with the truth, Gerald will not admit his guilt to Sheila directly- he avoids answering the direct question, "were you seeing her last spring and summer?" He wants to keep his relationship with Eva/Daisy from the Inspector, but, as Sheila understands, and says, "he knows" already; and he knows much more than they themselves know.

Gerald is like Mr Birling, in clinging to his belief ("I don't come into this suicide business"), and being slow to accept any responsibility for the consequences of his actions. He would rather suppress the truth than face it, and his casual approach to morality makes him slow to realise what an impact his dealings with Eva/Daisy must have on his plans to marry Sheila.

Act Two

The Inspector confirms that he has no more questions for Sheila, but has not finished asking questions. That means that she wants to stay, because (like the Inspector) she recognises the need to reach the truth.

Gerald wants to protect her from what is "bound to be unpleasant and disturbing" but, in saying this, he is perhaps mainly trying to protect himself from the damage the full revelation of his relationship with the "dead" girl will do to his relationship with Sheila. Just as he had done with Arthur Birling, the Inspector turns Gerald's words against him. She and Gerald both speak to each other "bitterly".

The Inspector elaborates on, and passes judgment on, Sheila's desire to stay; it is not that she wants to see others interrogated, he says, but that she needs to know how the responsibility is to be apportioned, and who else is to blame- otherwise, she will be "alone with her responsibility". He tells them- sternly- that "we have to share something...our guilt", meaning that if we, as individual people, are not prepared to share our wealth, and care for others less well off than us, we will have to share amongst ourselves the shame which comes from that choice.

Sheila stares at him, "wonderingly"; she seems to be the first of the characters to realise that he is not an ordinary police officer, but a figure with a mission to expose irresponsibility and lay bare the family's individual consciences.

Mrs Birling arrives "briskly and self-confidently" for her first conversation with the inspector. Her manner and attitude are very similar to her husband's. Sheila tells her that she is worried that her mother will say something she will regret; Mrs Birling rejects her daughter's point of view, just as her husband had dismissed Eric's.

The Inspector remarks that what he does often makes a stronger impression"on the young ones" (than on the older generation) - a hint that his purpose is to regenerate the morality of everyone who has a guilty conscience which they hide from themselves.

Mrs Birling is a cold snob, with a closed mind- which proves the Inspector's point. She thinks of Eva/Daisy as one of a group of "girls of that class", whom it is "absurd" to believe have any "feelings or scruples"- in other words, she views them as a sub-human species whose lives are ruled by simple appetites. In fact, it is the Eric Birlings and Gerald Crofts who fall short in this way.

She objects to the Inspector's manner, calling it "impertinent" and "offensive", and she tries to intimidate him with her husband's position in the community. These were the tactics Mr Birling had tried to use, without success.

Sheila is almost the Inspector's assistant here, confronting her mother with the fact of Eric's excessive drinking, which has been ongoing for two years, and which she should have been aware of.

Before he starts to question Mrs Birling, the Inspector confirms that he will want to question Eric too, but that he will have to wait. Mr Birling's objections align him with his wife against the probing alliance of Sheila and the Inspector. So, when the Inspector asks Gerald when he first knew Daisy Renton, only Mr and Mrs Birling are surprised. The Inspector wants Gerald's part in the story revealed before he moves on to Mrs Birling. Sheila is on a bitter quest to see whether she thinks Gerald really loves her and deserves to marry her.

Gerald had met Eva/Daisy at the bar in the Palace Variety Theatre- a place designated for prostitution ("it's a favourite haunt of women of the town"). Mr and Mrs Birling want to spare Sheila the details, but she wants the whole story, as she is "supposed to be engaged to the hero of it". Gerald is familiar with the location, and its "hard-eyed dough-faced women". Eva/Daisy stood out because "she was very pretty...soft brown hair and big dark eyes...young and fresh and charming and altogether out of place".

We are to take it that she was so desperate for money that she was prepared to resort to a life of prostitution, and had attracted the sleazy attention of Alderman Meggarty (another man whom Mrs Birling completely misjudges). Gerald rescued Eva/Daisy, took her to the County Hotel, bought her some food, offered her the use of his absent friend's rooms in Morgan Terrace for six months, gave her money to live on, and ("I suppose it was inevitable", he says) began a relationship with her, because she was "intensely grateful" and he felt sorry for her.

Sheila and the Inspector both want to know whether Gerald loved Daisy, so that they can judge how serious his betrayal of Sheila is. Although Mrs Birling calls it "this disgusting affair", in Edwardian society men who were not married did not cause a scandal when they had sex with prostitutes. Gerald says that the stronger feeling was Daisy's for him. Sheila is bitter and sardonic, but she applauds his honesty in admitting that he had felt flattered and important.

Priestley is interested in his characters' sexual morality as part of their overall social morality. An Edwardian audience (not, of course, that he wrote the play for one!) would have taken a different view of Gerald's values and behaviour from the original post-War audience. Possibly, a modern audience, influenced also by feminism and a stronger belief in equality and classlessness, takes a more critical view of Gerald; we wonder how he can seem to experience so little conflict over his betrayal of Sheila. We sympathise with her, because she seems by far the most modern character, in her outlook and her readiness to take responsibility for what she has done.

The play is set at a time when no women were entitled to vote in British elections. The Suffragettes were fighting against that – but many people in 1912, when this play was set, still felt it correct that only men could vote. By 1946, when this play was written all women over the age of 21 could vote.

Gerald ended the relationship in September 1911, and then Daisy/Eva had to vacate his friend's rooms. She had, we are told, enough money to live on for the remainder of the year. The Inspector says she went to the seaside for two months.

Gerald proposes to go for a walk, and this gives Sheila the opportunity to give him back the engagement ring; his behaviour has not been up to the standards she requires. She explains that she blames him for his lies and deceiving her, and that the evening's events have made them both different from how they were. She is certainly determined to be what she would call a better person; she is, no doubt, uncertain whether he is, too. Sheila refuses to let her father make excuses for Gerald, and tells him "don't interfere"!

Now it is Mrs Birling's turn to be inspected. She, like her husband, fails to recognise the identity of the girl at first. The Inspector accuses her of lying, and, when Mr Birling objects, he reminds him that he is "doing my duty" and that "public men...have responsibilities" (not to stand in the way of legitimate inquiries).

Interestingly, when Mr Birling says that the Inspector has not been sent "to talk to me about his responsibilities", the Inspector says he *hopes* he will not have to.

This means that it should be enough to make the family face what they have done; that most people would then (like Sheila) take their share of the blame, and adjust their values; but that he feels the Birlings may not be so honest.

Sheila confirms the Inspector's accusation that her mother is lying ("you did in fact recognise her, from the way you looked"). Mr Birling goes to see whether it is Eric or Gerald who has left, slamming the front door. This leaves the Inspector to confirm with Mrs Birling and Sheila that Mrs Birling chaired the recent meeting of the Brumley Women's Charity

Organization- only two weeks ago. She is evasive, but has to admit that she did; and that she saw Eva/Daisy, who applied for help, but did so calling herself "Mrs Birling".

It is just the kind of "impertinence" which, Mrs Birling admits, "prejudiced me against her". She confirms that she "didn't like her manner", but insists that "unlike the other three, I did nothing I'm ashamed of" and considers that "I did my duty". The Inspector tells her that she "did something terribly wrong", and which she will regret for the rest of her life, because the girl was pregnant-and Mrs Birling told her to go for support to the father of the child, because it was "his responsibility".

The Inspector says that she was seeking, not just money, but "advice, sympathy, friendliness", and Mrs Birling showed no compassion. Sheila calls this "cruel and vile". Mrs Birling insists that, as the child's father was known to her, he must be made responsible, and ought to be forced to marry her.

The Inspector tells Arthur Birling that he is "losing all patience with you people"- because Sybil Birling is so slow to recognise how wrong she was. He will not allow her not to make public (to the audience) what this woman had said- which was that her unborn child's father was a drunkard, young, silly and wild, and that neither of them would be served by marrying; and she would not take from him money which was not his.

Eva/Daisy's behaviour was nobler and more principled that Mrs Birling's; she wanted to protect the boy who had stolen the money he was giving her. Mrs Birling is adamant, though, ("it sounded ridiculous to me"), and she accepts "no blame for it at all".

In her view, the girl herself, and the "young man", were responsible; and if he came from a different (i.e. higher) class, then "he shouldn't escape. He should be made an example of." This would, of course, be precisely the sort of scandal which would torpedo Mr Birling's hopes of a knighthood. The irony which we are enjoying of course is that she is talking about her son (but doesn't know this) … and how different any mother would be if she knew it were her son!

Mrs Birling falls right into the trap. She says that, if he really was stealing to support her, the man in question is "entirely responsible" and ought to be punished. She says that the Inspector's duty is not to continue "asking quite unnecessary questions", but to make the man "confess in public his responsibility".

Priestley takes full drama from this moment.

First Sheila, then Arthur Birling, then Mrs Birling realise that it must be Eric they are talking about. As he comes on stage, looking extremely pale and distressed, the Act ends.

Act Three

Eric's drunken and irresponsible behaviour has emerged, not under questioning by the Inspector, but as a result of the other characters' knowledge and intuition. Mrs Birling is still in denial about her son's drink problem. Eric and her father both accuse Sheila of disloyalty; the Inspector insists that Eric must "tell me" what he has to say, and that he should be allowed more to drink, because as a man so dependent on it, he needs a little more just to enable him to function.

Eric met Eva/Daisy in November, in the Palace Theatre bar. As with Gerald, she was there as an apprentice prostitute, although, he says, "she wasn't the usual sort". Eric bought her drinks, was drunk himself (as usual), and forced his way into her lodgings. Over the next month or so, a casual relationship developed and she became pregnant; but she refused any idea of a marriage, because she knew that Eric did not love her. Eric had to support her, because she had no job and no money left; he took about £50 of the company's money.

Mr Birling is furious. Priestley uses words that include strong, animal feelings - anything but words that denote understanding. He is "explosive...very sharp...harsh...angry...savage". He asks Eric why he did not ask for help, and hears the devastating answer- "you're not the kind of father a chap could go to."

The final confession or revelation is the Inspector's, to Eric, that it was his own mother who turned Eva/Daisy away- which makes her guilty of murder and infanticide, in his view.

As a Birling family scuffle threatens to break out, the Inspector calls them to order. He sums up his findings in the manner of a detective in a country house murder mystery. Each of them played a part in the death of the girl. Mrs Birling showed no compassion at her time of need; she is cruel. Eric "used her" for his sexual gratification, and treated her as less than a person; he is gluttonous and lustful. Sheila was angry and envious. Mr Birling refused her pay claims, out of selfish greed. The Inspector absolves Gerald, because he cared for her "and made her happy for a time."

He tells Mr Birling that, in refusing a small pay rise and sacking her, he "made her pay a heavy price"; and now "she'll make you pay a heavier price still"- presumably, he means the forfeiture of his knighthood. Although none of them can apologise to the dead girl, they should remember that there are "millions and millions and millions" of others whose hopes and happiness depend on their interactions with us and on "what we think and say and do". In other words – always, all actions have consequences.

The Inspector's language in this final speech of his, with his references to "one body" and "blood and anguish", alludes to the Passion of Christ and to the Communion Service in the Christian faith. He repudiates completely the Birling parents' perspective; that we can or should stay secure and complacent, pleased with ourselves, behind our own front door.

On the contrary, he says that "we don't live alone… we are responsible for each other". His final warning is that, if we do not all learn that lesson, and adjust our behaviour, "we will be taught it in fire and blood and anguish"- a symbol for war, including the two World Wars, and also for revolution and civil war.

The Inspector leaves the other characters in a state of shock, and the recriminations start immediately. Mr Birling fears a "public scandal"; both he and his wife threaten to make Eric live a cleaner and more honest life. They are ashamed of *him*, but they refuse to accept that he is ashamed of *them*, and Sheila observes that her parents seem to have learned nothing, in that they are still refusing to accept any responsibility. Eric points out that his father would have categorised the Inspector as one of the cranks who say that we live in a community with everyone else.

Sheila is interested in the timing of the Inspector's arrival- at the very moment her father was expounding his anti-social doctrine of how 'it's every man for himself'- because she realises that he is not an orthodox policeman.

Mrs Birling is thinking the same thing. For the parents, who are seeking to evade their responsibility, this is a key point- it "makes all the difference". For Sheila, it is important in a different sense; their culpability is the same, but it clarifies the moral dimension. Eric shares Sheila's view; whether or not he was a police inspector, "he was our police inspector all right", the examiner of their consciences. Sheila echoes this a little later- "he inspected us all right", she says.

The parents say that the Inspector's language was not authentic; nor was his manner. While Eric has confessed to a criminal offence- theft- the other members of the family will be subjected to nothing worse than public humiliation.

Mr Birling observes that the Inspector was prejudiced and must be a "Socialist or some sort of crank". (He probably means 'and' rather than 'or' there, too). His wife expects her husband to "decide what we ought to do". But it is Gerald who returns, and confirms that "Inspector Goole" does not exist. Arthur Birling checks that information with the Chief Constable, and says, once more, that his bogus identity "makes all the difference", because the law has no power to punish them.

We see the parents regaining their self-satisfaction and complacency, and Mr Birling attributes the "hoax" to one of the (many) people in this town who dislike him. Gerald does not need, or wish, to know the full extent of Eric's sordid involvement.

Sheila and Eric object, again, to what they see as their parents trying to pretend that, because there are no tangible consequences, there has been nothing wrong. Mr Birling calls his own children's attitude "so damned exasperating"; all he can see is the private sphere and the public one.

As tempers fray, Gerald, who has aligned himself with the Birling parents throughout the play, asks the second crucial question – is it a fact that Eva/Daisy is dead?

There is no more proof of that than there is that the Inspector was real; there may have been more than one girl; they may not all have known the same one, or seen the same photograph.

Gerald ignores the fact that the Inspector has had access to the girl's diaries, and the two changes of name were enough in themselves to force guilt into the open. Mr Birling and Gerald question whether the suicide is real, and Gerald rings the hospital, to find that there has indeed been no death by disinfectant. Sheila points out that there may be no suicide, but that the sinful episodes and behaviours are still real.

Her father treats the whole "investigation" as a joke, and expects her to take Gerald's ring again; for him, the absence of consequences means the non-existence of guilt and no need for self-examination.

Sheila says that she finds it frightening that her parents will ignore the apocalyptic warning the Inspector left about social responsibility. Gerald offers her the ring again, saying that everything's all right now; she will not take it, because she needs time to think about what she wants to do.

Arthur Birling is in mid-sentence again, mocking Sheila's new, serious morality, when there is an incoming telephone call- announcing that "a girl has just died" on the way to hospital, and an Inspector is coming to investigate.

The third Act of the play is about evading responsibility, and reverting to old ways; change is essential, but hard.

Shocking people, by confronting them with their own bad behaviour, is not enough; we have to embrace the need for us to make the world a better place before anything can change.

The Inspector was right to lose patience with Arthur and Sybil Birling, and Gerald Croft is no better. A real revolution may be the only way to drag Britain out of its Edwardian complacency and into a modern, equality-based age.

Characters and their role in the play

Arthur Birling

Arthur Birling is a self-satisfied factory owner, a self-made man. He describes himself as "a hard-headed business man, who has to take risks and know what he's about". He is aged mid-fifties, "heavy-looking, rather portentous…rather provincial". His lack of sophistication and elegance comes over in his physique as well as the way he speaks. Although he is "prosperous", he still lives in "a fairly large suburban house", (so not a mansion, for example) which his wife Sybil, his "social superior", must feel is vulgar.

He is constantly looking for opportunities to improve his status and security. His intended son-in-law, Gerald, refers to his own father as "the governor", and he is abroad- perhaps he is the governor of a British colony overseas, and Gerald is already running the family business? Birling buys his port from the same merchant as Gerald's father, and he hopes to compensate for his undistinguished origins by receiving a knighthood, for his services as the former mayor of Brumley, as a magistrate, and as a "sound party man".

He sees a commercial opportunity in the marriage-
he hopes that, at some point, it is not just the
families which will intermarry, but that Crofts
Limited- older and bigger than Birling and Company
- will merge with his own company, in the interests
of synergy- of "lower costs and higher prices".

Mr Birling may be well off, but he is not well
educated, and his vocabulary is stubbornly lacking
in subtlety- he uses the phrase "very nice" three
times in his opening remarks. When he makes his
speech about the progress of the world, he repeats
himself and shows that he has no mastery of
language as well as little understanding of the world
-

("I just want to say this…And I want to say this…a
very good time…a very good time…a hard-headed
business man …a hard-headed, practical man of
business…we hard-headed practical business
men…a few German officers…begin talking
nonsense…a few German officers talking
nonsense…I'm telling you now…I tell you").

Priestley discredits him, using irony to show us that
Birling is a poor judge of the mood of the times. His
faith in new technology is blind; he says that the
"Titanic" is "unsinkable, absolutely unsinkable",
whereas we know that it hit an iceberg and sank on
its maiden voyage on 14 April 1912. He says that
there will not be a war, because "there's too much

at stake"; the First World War started in August 1914. Birling ends his speech with the clumsy and ironic misjudgement "we don't guess-we've had experience-and we know".

In fact, he knows very little, and understands less.

In his narrow view, progress is measured by advances in engineering. The message of the play is that progress is a social construct, not an industrial one. The social dimension is missing from Birling's world- he simply does not understand the "Socialist" view.

His instinct, in wanting to consolidate and protect his wealth and status, is defensive; he sees the world as a hostile and messy place, and he admits, in Act Three, that "there are people in this town who dislike me". He is alarmed by the idea, at the end of Act Two, that Eric is "mixed up" in the mess of Eva's death, just as he regards as "nonsense" the view of "these cranks" (socialists and leading thinkers of his day) that we are "all mixed up together like bees in a hive".

Arthur Birling manages to be abrasive, as well as pompous, small-minded and mean.

He thinks he can bully and intimidate the Inspector, through his connections (he plays golf with the chief constable, Colonel Roberts); he is willing to bribe him, with drink, or to pay money to avoid embarrassment, or to threaten to "report" him; and he suggests that the two of them should "go and talk this over quietly in a corner". All of these desperate gestures are futile in the face of the Inspector's quest for the truth, and they show how backward-looking Birling is.

He is almost childishly gleeful when he thinks that the Inspector is merely "a fake", because, to him, the man who has no social conscience, and no sense of social responsibility, it "makes all the difference".

The generation gap is very apparent in the angry confrontation which Birling begins with his own children, once the Inspector's authenticity is discredited. He uses clichés and doesn't listen to his children at all. He says that it is now time to "keep our heads…to behave sensibly", and he finds it "so damned exasperating" that Sheila and Eric "won't try to understand our position". He and his wife are not interested in the distinction between truth and public respectability which is so important to the Inspector and Sheila. However, he seems paranoid to us, as well as stupid and rather pathetic, in his relief that it is "all over now", and that Sheila should ask Gerald to give her the engagement ring again.

Birling has a particular issue with Eric. Gerald is the solid, capitalist, old-fashioned, reliable son he wishes he had had. Eric is the son he has. He contradicts Eric's request not to make a speech, tells him not to interrupt, patronises him ("you've a lot to learn yet") and addresses him as "my boy". He stares at Eric, and speaks to him sharply. He tells him "Don't get excited". He tells him to keep out of the discussion about the economics of wages, and says that, if Eric is ever to be able to make decisions, he will need to brighten his ideas and "face a few responsibilities" (this is ironic).

Arthur Birling resents the fact that the money he has spent on sending Eric to a public school and university appears to be paying no dividend; he thinks that his son is merely "spoilt". Eric collects money for the sales the company makes, but he has too little to do, and seems to operate in an alcoholic haze, which his father describes, euphemistically, as excitable queer moods. As Eric's involvement with Eva emerges in Act Three, Mr Birling speaks to him harshly and angrily, reacts "savagely" to Eric's confession of taking money (as if the company were not an inanimate thing but Mr Birling himself!), and calls him "a damned fool" and a "hysterical young fool". He has so little self-knowledge that he does not foresee that Eric could not ask him for help.

He blames Eric for the prospective scandal, and (again, ironically) accuses him of not caring about anything. He tells Sheila to keep her views to herself, and points out that no one will suffer more than him, when the events are reported publicly. Sheila attacks him for his obtuseness (he hasn't learnt anything) and Eric attacks him for his outlook ("it's every man for himself").

Birling is slow in thought as well as intelligence.

It is Sheila who feels first that there is something unauthentic about the Inspector; then he adopts the idea. It is Gerald who has checked his identity; then Birling confirms it with a call to Colonel Roberts. When Mrs Birling "looks expectantly" at him for a decision about what to do next, he cannot give a lead.

His reaction to his children's challenge to his moral authority is simply to tell them "you'd better keep quiet", and his behaviour towards Eric becomes "shouting, threatening". It is Gerald's idea that "Eva Smith" may not have been one girl, and may not be dead; Birling develops it, slowly at first, and then "eagerly" and "triumphantly". Birling mimics the Inspector, sarcastically, and points derisively at his own children, calling them "the famous younger generation who know it all".

Our response to Arthur Birling is frustration, not anger or pity. He is an obstacle to progress, an unevolved dinosaur. Priestley has presented him here in a way which reassures us that, with the passing of the Edwardian age- informed by our knowledge of the next 30 years' history- his species will become extinct. (You may, however, disagree with him. Can you think of people in society today who are similar to Mr Birling? Perhaps you can think of characters in films or books?)

For Priestley this is steering away from the topic. Mr Birling is the past. The more interesting question, for Priestley, is how can social responsibility be embedded in the values of all people, from every class and background?

Sybil Birling

The stage directions tell us that she is about 50, socially superior to her husband, and "rather cold". She certainly lacks empathy.

She has little to say in Act One; she gives instructions, to Edna, the parlour maid, to her husband ("you're not supposed to say such things", "I don't think you ought to talk business") and to her daughter ("don't tease him", "be careful").

She has an old-fashioned approach to the roles of men and women- she thinks it is fine that men "who have important work to do sometimes have to spend nearly all their time and energy on their business".

This of course is Gerald's cover for his summer of infidelity, which is one of the revelations to come, but it is hinted at, at the very start. Illogically, when Sheila raises the issue of Eric's drinking, she turns to Gerald, and says that because "you're a man" he "must know that it isn't true". Mrs Birling shares with her husband a dangerous complacency about their son, and an unpleasant assumption that, because of their position in the community, they are above investigation or criticism.

Despite being superficially bossy, Mrs Birling does not want to think for herself. When doubts arise about how the family can avoid a scandal, she waits for her husband to "decide what we ought to do".

Mrs Birling is on stage for the whole of Act Two, apart from the very start of it. She is self-confident, unreflective, and we soon see that she is a snob; she refers to Eva Smith disparagingly ("girls of that class", "a girl in her position") and refers to the whole investigation as "this absurd business".

She is "staggered" to hear of Alderman Meggarty's grubby sexual aggression towards Eva. She describes any information about extra-marital sex as "disgusting", but she has to apply the term to Gerald as well as Meggarty.

She feels that people should defer to her, so she is not impressed with the Inspector; she tells him he is "impertinent" and that his "manner" is "rather peculiar and offensive". When her husband is angry with the Inspector, she follows suit. Then, when the Inspector raises the charity committee meeting, she says that Eva/Daisy had "prejudiced me against her case" by calling herself "Mrs Birling", i.e. her name. She reacted to this "gross impertinence" by extracting a confession that the name "just happened to be the first she thought of".

Ironically, Mrs Birling demands that the young man who made Eva pregnant should be forced to marry her – if this had happened, Eva would indeed have become "Mrs Birling".

Sybil Birling's snobbishness and her lack of empathy are, together, a deadly combination. She tells the Inspector that Eva/Daisy "had only herself to blame", that her story was "quite false", and that in refusing her application because she "was not a good case" she did "nothing I'm ashamed of". She emphasises this by saying also that she was doing "my duty"; "nothing wrong"; "I was justified"; "I was perfectly justified"; "I accept no blame for it at all".

She had told Eva/Daisy to "go and look for the father of the child", because it was her business to make him responsible. He should "be compelled to marry her" or "at least support her". Eva/Daisy had said that because the father was young, silly, wild and drinking too much, it would be "wrong" for them both to marry, and that, because he had stolen the money he had given her, she would not take any more.

Mrs Birling blames Eva/Daisy for being working class, but at the end of Act Two she concedes that if the father of her unborn child "didn't belong to her class" it is even more important that "he shouldn't escape. He should be made an example of...he'd be entirely responsible...he should be made an example of".

At the start of Act Three she still refuses to accept that Eric has a drink problem ("you're not that type – you don't get drunk") because she cannot accept that her own son is a bad character. When Eric accuses her of killing Eva/Daisy, and her own grandchild, her defence is "I didn't know-I didn't understand". She will not apologise, or accept that she may have been in the wrong.

When doubts start to arise about the Inspector's role, she is "triumphant". She is still not remotely concerned about the rights and wrongs of what has happened, but only about whether there's "anything to be done about it" to prevent any repercussions for the family. She looks back at what she told the Inspector, not as a matter of telling the truth, but of how "I answered more or less as he wanted me to answer".

She grasps eagerly at the idea that, if the Inspector is not genuine, they can and indeed should go on behaving just as they always have.

She feels "amused" where she should feel contrite, ashamed of herself, and determined to become more compassionate and understanding. But her background- her social class and coldness- makes this impossible. She is insular, and she cannot see that she has any responsibility for the world beyond her own front door.

Apart from accepting that Eric should repay the money he "stole" from his father, she has no suggestions for change. She is simply relieved that the spotlight has moved on from her own sordid family. That is why the phone rings again and the (real?) Inspector is on his way.

We feel that Mrs Birling is insulated from the real world by her husband's wealth. She should be taking care of the Eva Smiths- she has the perfect opportunity to do so, through her position chairing the charity committee. But her class prejudice should really disqualify her from being in that position. In turning Eva/Daisy away, she is punishing her for being a pregnant, working class girl.

Being financially privileged but essentially stupid is not, Priestley is showing us, a harmless thing, because it affects everyone we encounter, and stands in the way of the social cohesion we need.

If Mrs Birling were a casualty of the revolution the Inspector talks about in his final speech, there would be few tears shed. Priestley has drawn Mrs Birling as the damning embodiment or archetype of what is obnoxious in the upper class. She is preoccupied with her own status, sees no evil, and hears no evil. She does not listen and is incapable of humility, self-examination, or improvement.

Gerald Croft

Gerald is described as "an attractive chap about 30, the easy well-bred young man-about-town." Gerald is- to Mr Birling in particular- a desirable son-in-law, because he is superior socially, and offers the prospect of a business as well as a family merger (Mr Birling sees things in financial terms, and has an eye for making his family, like his business, more secure and profitable).

Both Mr and Mrs Birling trust Gerald. They think that his breeding is a guarantee of integrity. It is not. At the start of the play, he repeats an ongoing lie to

Sheila- that he paid little attention to her the previous summer because he was too busy at work. He is not only unfaithful to his fiancée but is untrustworthy.

His manners are polite, and he seems to be completely respectable. Mr Birling confides in him his hopes of a knighthood, as a way of ingratiating himself socially. When he says that the only thing that could prevent it is a scandal, Gerald offers the opinion "you seem to be a nice well-behaved family". We come to see that he emphasis here is, ironically, on the word *seem* – the Birlings are in fact all defective, and not what they seem to be; but neither is Gerald.

Gerald is in Mr Birling's confidence in a way his own son, Eric, is not. Eric may feel troubled and excluded by this preferential treatment of an outsider.

When the Inspector arrives, in Act One, Gerald asks to be excused from the investigation of the family's behaviour, but, when the Inspector hears that Gerald "hopes to marry" Sheila, he says that he must stay.

He continues to make supportive noises which agree with Mr Birling's attitude to sacking the striking factory workers ("you couldn't have done anything else…I know we'd have done the same thing"). He is polite but firm with the Inspector, refusing to be deferential, but when the name Daisy Renton is mentioned he is "startled" and needs a drink of whisky; the Inspector refers back to this moment as the one where Gerald gave himself away.

Sheila realises, at the end of Act One, that Gerald had been seeing "Daisy Renton" when he claimed to be working so hard. His response to being confronted with the truth is worth paying attention to. He apologises to Sheila, and tries to persuade her that they can "keep it from" the Inspector, and when she tells him he is a "fool"- because the Inspector knows much "that we don't know yet"- he looks "crushed". His duplicitous and complacent way of life, and his lack of faithfulness, will – quite rightly- jeopardise his plans to marry Sheila.

They are left on their own at this dramatic moment, and then Act Two starts with the Inspector returning. He is sarcastic towards Gerald now - "you think young women ought to be protected against unpleasant and disturbing things?". Gerald would like Sheila to leave the discussion- perhaps because he wants to keep from her the sordid details of his relationship with Daisy. He and Sheila exchange bitter and stressful remarks, before the Inspector takes charge and tells Gerald that Sheila wants to stay because she needs to feel that the responsibility for Eva's suicide is shared, rather than just hers.

Gerald informs Mrs Birling about Eric's reputation as a drinker in the wider world ("I have gathered that he does drink pretty hard"). Then he is made to recount how he knew Daisy. He says he met her in the bar at the theatre in Brumley. He tries, again, to persuade Sheila to leave the discussion; rightly, she insists that she wants to hear the explanation of his behaviour towards "the girl he's supposed to be in love with".

He explains that what attracted his attention was Daisy's "soft brown hair and big dark eyes". (Sheila, we are told in the stage directions at the start of the play, "is a pretty girl in her early twenties" - her colouring is not mentioned) and the fact that she was "young and fresh and charming". He has a rather unconvincing moment of distress when he says he realises that she has died; it passes in an instant.

He says that he rescued her from the grasp of the lascivious Alderman Meggarty, who had "wedged her into a corner", and took her to the County Hotel for a drink and a conversation- "a little friendliness". When he discovered she had no money and no food, and was about to be evicted from her rented room, he moved her into some rooms a friend of his had made available to him while he went to Canada for six months- but without any designs on her. "I was sorry for her" is how he puts it.

Gerald's explanation of how a good deed turned into an affair is weak- with the emphasis on how attractive he found her, and her gratitude to him, we see that it was always going to happen-

"she was young and pretty and warm-hearted…intensely grateful…it was inevitable." Asked, by Sheila and the Inspector, whether he was in love with Daisy, he remains non-committal – "it's hard to say". He refuses to elaborate on precisely how often he saw her. He is "troubled" now because when he ended the relationship, she was not bitter, but "said she'd been happier than she'd ever been before".

When he asks to be allowed to go out for a walk, Sheila gives him back the engagement ring he had given her earlier in the play. This gives him time to reflect, and he returns after some time for the final part of Act Three, to assert that he is "almost certain" that the Inspector "wasn't a police officer", because he had happened to meet a police sergeant who told him there was no such man in the local force. This means that the investigation is a con- he uses the words 'we've been had' and Mr Birling uses the same phrase after he phones the chief constable to confirm that there is no Inspector Goole.

Gerald suggests that there may have been no suicide (although his affair with Daisy was real). Then he is the character who realises that it is possible that Eva Smith and Daisy Renton are two different girls, and that the photos the Inspector showed Sheila and her father and her mother may have been different. He even says that "there were probably four or five different girls" (one to fit each person's scenario, in fact); and, if so, there was probably no suicide, which they can check by phoning the hospital.

We may be caught up in the tension here, but Priestley will not let it slacken. So no one suggests the common sense solution of each person describing the girl each of them had known, so that they could establish whether it was the same person or not.

Instead we have the tantalising poser, is it one girl; is it lots of girls … and then we continue with the plot.

Even stupid Mr Birling thinks "it will look a bit queer" ringing the hospital so late in the evening, but Gerald volunteers to make the call. He and Birling adopt the same attitude; the fact that the suicide is an invention means that "everything's all right now, Sheila". Gerald invites her to reinstate their engagement but she says it is too soon for that.

Our first instinct is to align Gerald with Sheila, and, perhaps, to give him the benefit of the doubt; to assume that he has learnt a lesson he will not forget. But this is not justified. He apologises to Sheila when there is no possibility of keeping his infidelity a secret. His attitude towards the rights of employees and the duty of employers is identical to Arthur Birling's. He may be (slightly) more intelligent than the Birlings, none of whom seems at all bright, and his initial involvement with Eva/Daisy was unselfish. But he will not accept responsibility, or adjust his values, or learn a lesson.

Gerald is the keenest to discredit the Inspector, first by checking with the police whether the Inspector is on their staff, and then by checking deaths at the hospital. He feels- rightly- that his future with Sheila is at stake. He assumes- wrongly- that if the Inspector's case is invented, everything can be as it was- he can still marry Sheila. But this would be to ignore his misbehaviour, and to apply no punishment or consequences to it.

Sheila's conscience will not allow her to ignore Gerald's infidelity; her father tries to brush it aside as normal male behaviour, but Sheila objects to being lied to; she wants the "honest" truth, however unpalatable it may be, and she will not compromise her values in order to settle for less than a proper, exclusive, relationship.

Gerald may be relatively young (about 30), but he is too like Mr Birling to be part of the solution; he is really part of the problem, because he sees the working class as beneath him (there was no possibility of marrying Daisy/Eva) and he will always excuse his own behaviour, however bad. It is his suggestion that "everything is all right now" which is contradicted, and corrected, by the second ringing of the phone at the end of the play; because they are all still in denial about the seriousness and consequences of their selfish, exploitative behaviour, they will have to be put through another investigation-to see whether they will accept any responsibility the second time round.

Eric Birling

Eric has been educated at public school and university. He seems to be a disappointment to his father, even before his drunkenness and its consequences become clear.

Before he even speaks, Eric laughs, near the start of the play, when Sheila complains that Gerald had ignored her, and Gerald says he "will be careful"-careful, that is, to keep his real activities secret. Sheila accuses him of laughing because he is drunk; he denies it. Sheila calls him an "ass" and a "chump".

Eric does not want to have to listen to a long speech by his father, because he resents him for his coldness and distance. When the speech comes, he challenges his father's optimism, asking "What about war?" He is more aware than his parents of what is going on in the wider world.

He stops himself from saying something which would betray his involvement with Eva Smith. His father is treating Gerald as if he were his son, and Eric has been excluded from their private conversation about the possible knighthood. When the Inspector rings the doorbell, and Gerald jokes that the visit may be because "Eric's been up to something", he is uneasy- because Eva is pregnant with his illegitimate child- although the real reason for his edginess is not clear to the audience at the time.

His father constantly tells Eric to be quiet, and keep out of the conversation. When Mr Birling tells the Inspector about the strike and Eva's dismissal, Eric points out that he could have kept her on, and that the idea that anyone can simply find another job is simplistic; losing your job might be the start of a process which leads eventually to suicide. Then he says that workers should be able to negotiate, and that having "more spirit than the others" should not single you out for dismissal as a troublemaker.

Like Gerald, he says he has never known an Eva Smith. He asks to be allowed to go to bed because he has a headache and has been drinking, but the Inspector won't agree. Eric's contribution to Act One is three speeches of four or five lines, and thirty-one speeches of two lines or less- he is treated very much as a small child, ignored, discouraged from contributing, and not listened to.

While Eric is out of the room, in Act Two, Gerald tells Mrs Birling and Sheila about Eric's reputation as a "pretty hard drinker". It is this characteristic which makes his relationship with Daisy so sordid- he cannot remember anything about their first encounter. Absent throughout Act Two, he only appears at the very end of it, where he has no lines, but looks "extremely pale and distressed". We already know that he is the father of Eva's unborn child, and that his mother insists that he should be punished for that – "made an example of", "dealt with very severely", "compelled to marry" her and "compelled to confess in public his responsibility".

Eric's "confession" opens Act Three. It is as bad, dissolute, undignified and pathetic as Gerald's, but even more so, because his involvement with Eva was completely selfish, and the product of drunkenness, not concern for her. But he is subjected to a long sequence of twenty-seven questions, with his own father ganging up with the Inspector and adding his criticisms over the "theft" of money from his office.

Eric's bad behaviour is inexcusable, but his parents' attitude towards him has been deplorable, so that he now articulates the problem; his father is "not the kind of father a chap could go to when he's in trouble", and his mother " never did...understand anything". Mr Birling is exasperated with Eric, dismisses his ideas contemptuously, and refuses him a meaningful or responsible job in running the family business, while Mrs Birling is blissfully unaware of his drink problem. They are neglectful and cold parents, and Eric's frustration and rootlessness motivates his irresponsible, self-indulgent behaviour.

Stage directions indicate Eric's tone of voice- he speaks "sulkily", "quietly, bitterly", "angrily", "defiantly", and "bursting out". He is explosive because he can see and feel that the world outside his stuffy parents' home is beckoning him, but he is ill equipped to be effective or successful in it.

While Eric is not an attractive character, his unattractiveness reflects badly on the parents who have made such a poor job of bringing him up. He supports Sheila in confronting his parents' denials of responsibility or the need for change; he is "ashamed" of them, and of his father's concerns about his knighthood, and his authoritarianism generally. But Eric is an unhappy, rebellious young man, not a leader who can drive forward reform. He lacks his sister's capacity for clear thought.

Sheila Birling

It may seem odd, but the 50-year-old Priestley enlists the young, excitable and spoilt character of Sheila as the voice of conscience and guilt. Two things stand out in her speeches- the number of questions she asks (which serve to reinforce the sense of discomfort, because the Inspector knows everything in advance of the various characters' "confessions") and the morality of her language.

Sheila is exuberant, and happy about her engagement to Gerald, although she is suspicious of his unexplained lack of interest in her during the past summer. Her rather tearful affection for him turns to contempt and then respect, because at least he is honest about his bad behaviour.

Once she has been given the engagement ring, Sheila goes off-stage until the Inspector has arrived. When she reappears, she is disturbed by the contrast between her own happiness and the "horrible" death of Eva Smith.

When the Inspector confirms that Eva was young and pretty, it conveys to us that it is an accident of birth which put Sheila and Eva into their respective positions. She herself sees the photo, realises that the girl she complained about is the dead girl, and runs out crying.

She returns, to admit that she complained about Eva because "I was in a furious temper" and because she knew that the girl would have looked better than Sheila did in a particular dress. The Inspector defines Sheila's motive as jealousy.

Sheila accepts that she is "responsible" for Eva's death, and she promises that she had never behaved like this before, and never will again. We see her revenge against the sales assistant as petty and immature, and the word she used in her complaint- "impertinent"- is the same snobbish term her mother uses to dismiss Eva's claim for help to her charity. When Mrs Birling accuses the Inspector (in Act Two) of being impertinent, Sheila defines it as "such a silly word"; she has put aside her own silliness, and become serious. Her language becomes less emotional and superficial, and more judgmental and objective.

Act One ends with Gerald reluctantly admitting that Sheila's intuition- that he was involved with Eva- is correct. In Act Two, she observes the questioning of Gerald, her mother and Eric, because, although she accepts her own share of the blame, she cannot bear all of the responsibility herself.

From the start of Act Two, Sheila's language is full of moral/legal terminology- she uses words that include clear meanings such as "blame", "fault", "true"," sorry", "trouble"," honest"," excuse" and " admit it". After the Inspector leaves (early in Act Three) she takes over his role, in not allowing her family to evade their responsibility, and forcing them to accept the consequences of their actions.

She argues that it does not matter whether or not the Inspector is real; the point is that her parents are being "childish" and "don't seem to have learnt anything". They are "trying not to face the facts."

Sheila then uses the language of death by hanging for murder. She says the Inspector is "giving us rope – so that we will hang ourselves" that "he made us confess" and that "we're all in it up to the neck" because of "our crimes and idiocies". Sheila uses such serious language because she recognises how serous their wrongdoing has been.

Her last few speeches are full of frustration and fear, because her parents will not "learn", but will "go on in the same old way", being "cruel and vile" to those of a lower social class and those in need.

As one of the "young ones" whom the Inspector finds more "impressionable", Sheila is receptive to the need for change in a way the other characters are not. Her characterisation makes the point that necessary social change will only be possible if we adjust our private morality first. That means not just taking responsibility for our own mistakes, but challenging the selfishness and insularity of others. It is because Sheila's parents (and Gerald) refuse to be shaken out of their complacency, first by the Inspector's final, apocalyptic speech, and then by her challenge, that the dramatic second phone call occurs at the end of the play.

Inspector Goole

The Inspector is a "massive", portentous and rather lugubrious presence. His name (a pun on "ghoul" or ghost) and his unnatural staring and mannerisms imply that he is human in some ways, but not in others; he is a ghost of conscience; he knows everything; his purpose is to establish guilt, not in order to punish it, but to force the guilty to reform their values, their behaviour and their morality.

He tells Gerald that he finds it difficult to define the line which separates respectable citizens from criminals. The precise meaning of this is open to interpretation. It may mean that everyone has the capacity to do bad things; and/or that the apparently respectable are particularly interested in maintaining appearances, while they are as much criminals as anybody else.

He tells Mr Birling that "public men"- such as factory owners and magistrates- have "responsibilities as well as privileges". Judged by the Inspector's standards, the Birlings have not done what it was reasonable to expect from them.

His arrival- at the very moment where Arthur Birling is expounding his doctrine of individualism (or selfishness)- is calculated and deliberate, as if it is this creed (the creed of greed) which he goes about challenging. We feel that the Inspector- who belongs to no local police force- will knock on the door of all families like the Birlings, in order to influence "the young ones" to dismantle the old thinking, and usher in the era of "community", so that the millions of John Smiths and Eva Smiths do not face the same fate as Eva.

The Inspector refuses a drink on the grounds that he is "on duty", and at the end of Act Two he tells Mrs Birling that he is "waiting…to do my duty".

His duty is to dismantle the other characters' belief that they have no social responsibility and that their actions have no consequences for others.

He exists to blow up their complacency, by exposing it and making them face the implications of what they are and what they have done. Then he will leave them to "adjust their relationships".

He confronts Mr Birling's attempts to evade responsibility for Eva's death by putting forward his own theory- that Mr Birling's actions set about a dire chain of events, culminating in suicide-

"what happened to her then may have determined what happened to her afterwards, and...may have driven her to suicide".

He also contradicts Birling's (and Gerald's) attitude to the strikers by giving the opinion that "it's better to ask for the earth than to take it" – meaning that if people cannot secure what they need by consent, they will have no choice but to take it by force.

This comment links with the Inspector's final speech (early in Act Three) which is both quasi-religious ("we are members of one body") and pseudo-revolutionary.

Eric reminds Mr Birling that the Inspector is "one of those cranks" who believe not in individualism but in collectivism (the "hive" which Birling talked about in his speech, and dismissed as "nonsense"). It is clear that the Inspector wants to see hope, financial security and comfort distributed more evenly. He says that if nothing else can be shared then the

Birlings and Sheila will have to share their guilt because "we have to share something".

In Act Three, he tells Mr Birling "you'll be able to divide the responsibility between you when I've gone". He is clear and unambiguous: responsibility rests with them all, it is only a matter of how much of the total responsibility each one bears that merits discussion.

The Inspector's questioning becomes more aggressive as the play progresses. He is much gentler with Sheila and Gerald than with Mrs Birling and Eric. At regular intervals, he emphasises the feelings Eva Smith had, as her fortunes became bleaker and bleaker, so that the Birlings have to think beyond their own complacent and comfortable life- he says it would be good for us to "put ourselves in the place of these young women, counting their pennies in their dingy little back bedrooms". As "cheap labour", they are unable to save for the future or to improve their semi-skilled, exploited lives, no matter how hard they work.

It is this lack of empathy for the poor who inhabit the same town as them which makes the Birlings so objectionable. Mrs Birling tells the Inspector that it was "simply absurd" for Eva to talk about "feelings and scruples" because of her "position"- she thinks that working-class girls have no feelings at all. This class prejudice leads the inspector to tell her that he is "losing all patience with you people".

He goes on to address each of the "suspects" in turn, having imposed order on them when they are about to start coming to blows. He instructs them "to remember" and "never forget" that they "helped to kill" Eva (Arthur Birling later mimics this part of his speech, sarcastically); their crimes of conscience make them accessories to murder/suicide.

Each of the Birlings had treated Eva inhumanely, as if she was "an animal, a thing, not a person" (he excuses Gerald, who was fond of her and made her happy). The Inspector leaves the Birlings with the moral that, because there are millions of people like Eva- the economically weak, working poor- those, like the Birlings, who can ease their "suffering" or promote their "happiness", have a responsibility or duty to treat them properly.

He ends his time on stage by warning that, if this lesson is not learnt, there will be dire consequences – he uses the words, "fire and blood and anguish". This is not a direct reference to any one specific event, although we may see it as prophetic of both World Wars; it may also refer to revolution, specifically socialist-led revolution, which makes more sense here, as he is talking about social equality at home, not international or global conflict.

Sheila had responded to the Inspector's doctrine of sharing guilt (in Act Two) by "staring at him ...wonderingly" and telling him that there is something about him she does not understand. After he leaves, she is sensitive to the timing of his arrival- timed so that he could discredit the doctrine of individualism- and she senses that he may not be a real policeman.

She has understood that it is the *motivation* for their behaviour that excuses or condemns them; her parents think that if there are no illegalities, the consequences of their behaviour can be ignored.

<u>To Eric and Sheila, the authenticity of the Inspector is of no importance; their consciences have been inspected, they have had to face their guilt, and they will not behave in the same way in the future.</u>

 For their parents, and Gerald, his identity is all that matters; if they have been tricked or bluffed, there is no responsibility to accept or blame to deal with; and no need to do anything differently. The clearest example of this is the assumption that Sheila will instantly reinstate her engagement to Gerald.

She could; she is free to do so; but it would go against her conscience, and, morally, his infidelity remains an issue (despite the Edwardians' tacit acceptance of prostitution for young unmarried men, provided it was a private activity).

Sheila grasps the fact that, although the Inspector asked them questions, there was no information which he did not know beforehand. A criminal investigation involves assembling the truth from small scraps of information provided by various informants. But this Inspector knew the facts before he started the enquiry!

Only Sheila understands the true, metaphysical aspect of the Inspector. He is the catalyst for greater understanding and greater humanity. The fact that his credentials are false- that he is not exactly who or what he says he is- enables the Birling parents and Gerald to try to persuade themselves that they have had a lucky escape and that he is a hoaxer perpetrating some kind of joke. This is both paranoid and the product of an inflated sense of their own importance. But their attitude is cowardly and compromised, because they are looking for ways of excusing themselves. The Inspector has the power to extract a confession of guilt from each of them, but not to pass a prison sentence; they have to agree to reform themselves, and only Sheila and (possibly) Eric will do this.

The Inspector still has the last word, in that, when his serious moral message fails to hit home, the telephone rings, to repeat the whole uncomfortable process. Therefore it does not matter whether the Inspector and the suicide are "real" or not.

Sheila and Eric are right; he is the Inspector not of crime and punishment but of guilty consciences and responsibility.

Eva Smith

Medieval morality plays- the earliest surviving form of drama in the English language- often featured a character called Everyman, whose soul was fought over by other characters- virtues, vices, angels. Eva Smith is an archetype too- she stands for every member of the working poor, semi-skilled or unskilled, male or female. In England in 1912 there were 10 million such people, and the threat of strikes was growing; not with the aim of a social revolution, but simply for them to have enough money each week to house, clothe and feed themselves and their dependants.

The Inspector is, at the same time, a physical human being (though a slightly odd one) and a spiritual and moral force (a ghoul). Eva may or may not be dead; she belongs, properly, in a ghost story, as she haunts the action of the play. But she is not an evil spirit. She embodies a romanticised, noble concept of the humble labourer very similar to Steinbeck's portrayal of the dignified, unselfish but desperately poor agricultural labourer in the

American dust bowl in his novels "Of Mice and Men" and "The Grapes of Wrath".

Just as a thin line separates the respectable citizen from the criminal, a similarly fine distinction discriminates between the privileged (Sheila) and the underprivileged (Eva). Both girls are in their early twenties, lively and pretty, and high-spirited. Sheila can look forward to a respectable marriage, and a comfortable and leisurely life, with children and servants. Eva lost two jobs, because the Birlings were vile/cruel/ spiteful/vindictive towards her. Then she was sexually used and abused by Gerald and Eric; became a prostitute; became pregnant; and was refused any charitable support by Sybil Birling, so that her suicide killed the Birlings' grandchild.

Eva's desperate predicament comes to us through the mouthpiece of the Inspector, who says he has not only a photo of the dead girl but a letter and a "sort of diary". The key fact is that she allowed Eric to take no responsibility for her and their child (which would have brought about the very scandal Arthur Birling is so keen to avoid); she decided it would be wrong to make him marry her because of his drunken mistake, although she could then have achieved some security for herself and her unborn baby.

She preferred to sacrifice herself than to compromise Eric, although she was more decent than him. She would not take any more stolen money from him. Instead, she subjected herself to the final humiliation of being patronised, condemned, preached at and rejected by Sybil Birling and the "charity" she represents.

Regardless of the personal cost, Eva will not take advantage of other people, or exploit their mistakes or vulnerability. How she treats Eric is a stark contrast to how Sheila treats her, and how Arthur Birling treats her. She has a generous and forgiving nature; theirs is mean and punitive.

In Charlotte Bronte's "Jane Eyre", Jane's saintly and long-suffering friend Helen Burns dies; Jane is spared. Helen becomes Jane's inspiration, as she makes her own way in the world, bears suffering with patience, and forgives those who cause her what the inspector calls "offence". Eva Smith should be to the Birlings what Helen is to Jane Eyre; a ghostly model of humanity. Sheila is young enough and impressionable enough to learn the lesson, partly because, but for an accident of birth, she might have been Eva, and Eva her; but her parents will not.

A harsh critic of Eva would say that she is too supine; instead of going to the seaside to prolong the memory of happiness she had found with

Gerald, she should have been more assertive, and not allowed Eric to exploit her. But her previous experience of asserting herself- as a leader of the group demanding higher pay for Birling's workers- had ended badly; he had punished her, made an example of her, and sacked her.

Because the Inspector stresses that there are millions of John Smiths and Eva Smiths, whose prospects of happiness or misery depend on others in their communities, we understand that the uneven encounter between the all-powerful Birlings and the powerless Eva is symbolic of a social struggle. This is not so much the struggle of the working class vs the middle class, or socialism vs capitalism, as between the clear conscience and the guilty conscience, the exploited and the exploiters, the privileged few and the underprivileged many.

Priestley insists, through the character of Eva, that when humanity encounters inhumanity, then humanity will eventually, despite overwhelming odds, win through. He sees the re-engineering of British society, after the Second World War, as a means of protecting all the surviving and future generations of Evas from the patronising and uncaring older Birlings.

Taking it further: looking for themes and strong essays

You should now feel that you understand both the plot (or narrative) of the play, and the characters. But there is another means of giving a play unity- the continuity of themes.

Where you can detect **recurring themes**, you will almost certainly **find meaning**.

You may be able to find some more of your own, but now let's have a look at some of Priestley's favourite themes, which help to unify the mood and action of the play.

In particular, we will look at:

* notions of crime and sin

* theories of time

* the language of snobbishness and chauvinism

* respectability and scandal.

Crime and sin

Sheila tells Gerald that the Birling family has committed a collection of crimes and idiocies- but the line between illegality and immorality is hard to define. It is helpful to think of the Birlings' behaviour in terms of the seven deadly sins- they are, after all, sins which have apparently led to a death.

The seven deadly sins are: wrath, greed, sloth, pride, lust, envy and gluttony.

In addition, the Old Testament text Proverbs 6: 16-19 itemises "seven things the Lord hates"- haughtiness or pride, lying, murder or hands that shed innocent blood, plotting evil, eagerness to do wrong or feet that are swift to run into mischief, a false witness who utters lies, and sowing discord.

And, in Galatians 5:19-21, St Paul sets out a list of sins which will disqualify anyone from inheriting the kingdom of God- "sexual immorality, impurity and debauchery....hatred, discord, jealousy, fits of rage, selfish ambition....envy, drunkenness, orgies....".

This could almost be an extract from the Birling family calendar! It reminds us that "An Inspector Calls" is not just about caring for others; it is about saving ourselves, as well as the society we are part of, from the damage of personal immorality.

The play does not calibrate degrees of guilt among the individual Birlings. Both the Inspector and these lists of wrongs excuse Gerald, up to a point. Who is most responsible for the death of Eva Smith? The blame and responsibility should be shared, because, as the Inspector says, each of them contributed to "the chain of events".

Mrs Birling, who is haughty, a liar, and eager to do wrong (to Eva/Daisy, whom she finds "impertinent"), is also guilty of the infanticide of her own grandchild, according, at least to Eric- although he is lustful and gluttonous in his sexual behaviour and drinking.

Arthur Birling is greedy, periodically angry, proud, envious of the Croft family's superior social position.....Sheila is wrathful and envious......

I recommend that you spend some time analysing, in turn, which character is guilty of which sins. Does that affect how you judge them, individually, and as a group?

I think they have a collective guilt for "sowing discord" because of their reluctance to involve themselves with the mass of humanity and the struggle against poverty just outside their closed front door.

Which of the characters is most "eager to do wrong"? Is it Arthur Birling, in his overriding desire to avoid scandal and his greed for a knighthood?

Or could it be Sheila, with her malicious and vindictive abuse of her power? Perhaps you would suggest Gerald, with his slippery morality towards his fiancée, and his complacent, patrician capitalism?

Whatever their (many) individual faults, what unites the characters in guilt is their absence of compassion for those less wealthy or secure than themselves- their deliberate lack of care.

Theories of time

One of Priestley's interests was the notion that there may be more to time than our perception of it. He was influenced by the philosopher JW Dunne, who thought that our dreams may reveal that we know future events before they occur and we experience them.

The Inspector is, in some sense, a time traveller. He has seen Eva Smith's diary and suicide letter; he is sure of some of his facts (but not all); he is investigating a tragedy which seems not to have taken place yet, although he presents it in starkly realistic terms (dwelling on the agony of poisoning by disinfectant).

He despairs of Arthur and Sybil Birling, because of their resistance to confronting their own guilt and responsibility. Sheila becomes his assistant, in anticipating how he will get Mrs Birling to condemn herself, and in seeing the signs that he is not an orthodox or real police officer.

It is only after Mr Birling is celebrating the family's escape from the threat of scandal (because no death at the hospital means no news story, no inquest and no publicity) that the telephone rings again, to announce that a girl has died and an Inspector is on his way.

The older Birlings' refusal to learn the lesson of their social responsibility, and their culpability for the poverty and suffering of the people they patronise and exploit, means that they must relive the investigation- so that they can have another opportunity to "adjust", to borrow the Inspector's term.

The family needs, finally, to make the connection between their avowed horror and shock at Eva's death and their own ability to prevent it. Can they still apologise to Eva Smith? Has she died or hasn't she? If she has, are they ready to atone for their role in her death by treating the other millions of John Smiths and Eva Smiths in a kinder and more humane way? Or will they, as Eric did to Eva, still treat the rest of the world as "an animal, a thing, not a person", even after the Inspector has pointed out that "we are members of one body"?

It is interesting that we feel that a second chance may still not be enough for the older generation. There have been two World Wars; two visits by an Inspector; two apparent suicides. Symbolically, Priestley is aligning war with suicide, and asking us how we remodel the society which survives these traumas.

Another symbolic meaning or dimension comes out of Priestley's treatment of time. It seems odd (though helpful to the dramatic tension) that the

Inspector starts to insist that he hasn't much time, when he has been laborious in the earlier part of his questioning.

1912 marked the emergence of the earliest form of the welfare system in Britain. A Pensions Act in 1908 had provided small pensions for a narrow group of very elderly citizens; in 1911, National Insurance was introduced, so that unemployed and ill people received a small temporary income, funded partly by the government and by other taxpayers. Any form of social insurance depends on the principle that we have a collective responsibility for each other- which is precisely the point Priestley's Inspector insists on.

The old Victorian idea, that self-sufficiency or the workhouse would do, had become unsustainable, because the processes of production- in agriculture as well as manufacturing- were becoming less labour-intensive, so that there was growing unemployment among the unskilled and uneducated. The Birling parents are symbolic of the Victorian values of enterprise, individuality, the work ethic, capitalism, and independence; Sheila and Eric acknowledge the new social reality that the poor cannot be left to be victimised and starved. The years immediately after the Second War saw the welfare system extended; the school leaving age raised to 15 in 1947; the National Health Service was set up in 1948.

Unless and until people like Arthur and Sybil Birling come to see that despite inequalities in income and wealth, every citizen deserves a decent education, access to health care, and a basic entitlement to welfare, making meaningful change will be difficult.

The Liberal Government had found this out in the years before 1912 when, despite offering such reforms, not enough people voted for them; Priestley's play is a plea in 1946 for the better-off to accept the financial costs of creating a fairer society which protects the weak from exploitation.

Time was short because there would not be another opportunity to reboot society, after two World Wars. Priestley may have felt, as he turned 50, that the chance would not arise again in his lifetime. That is why the Inspector is in a hurry, and why he becomes so impatient with Mr and Mrs Birling.

Whether or not the downfall and suicide of Eva/Daisy is really true, she stands for the oppressed working class and her story shows why the safety net of a welfare state is necessary. It was losing her two jobs in 1910- before the protection of any system of National Insurance- which started the fatal "chain of events" and allowed her to fall into the hands of the exploitative men- Gerald and Eric- who treat her largely as a sex object, and abuse her. The wealth, leisure, power and selfish amorality of the richer allows them to do to the poor what Eric in particular does to Eva/Daisy.

It may not be illegal, but it is morally indefensible, and so such behaviour- and the lack of values which lie behind it- is "criminal".

The ending of the play raises some intriguing possibilities. Has there now been a real suicide, because the Birlings' response to the imagined suicide was inadequate? Or is the play a "precognition" of an event which was always bound to happen? Or, again, is the latest death as unreal as the one the Inspector was investigating? Perhaps the most satisfying interpretation is that, because the older Birlings and Gerald have tried to excuse themselves, in Act Three, because there has been no death, they will now be confronted with a repeat, but without the possibility this time of evading the consequences of their selfishness.

The language of snobs and chauvinists

Priestley wants to make his play highly realistic so that he can give the unrealistic elements – the identity and purpose of the Inspector, and the ambiguity over the reality of the suicide- more dramatic weight. One of the key elements in realism is the language of the characters.

Priestley was aged 16 in 1912, and his father was a middle-class teacher, so we would expect him to have an ear for the language of the time, and the Birling family is of his own social class.

It is difficult for us to judge how antiquated the language he puts into their mouths is, in 1946, but "squiffy", "Steady the Buffs!", and "By Jingo!" - expressions that the characters use in the play- do seem to belong to an earlier age.

However, the real interest for a modern audience is in other aspects of the characters' language. It is probably both authentic, and it also suits Priestley's purpose, that he can show his class-conscious characters being demeaning, or derogatory, about the female gender in general and about Eva Smith in particular.

He manages the characters' language, so that, while we are critical of the Birlings' values and behaviour, we recognise that part of the issue is the time they live in.

While the Inspector refers to Eva, repeatedly, as either "this girl", "the girl", and "this young woman" and "a young woman", Gerald and the Birlings very rarely allow her the dignity of womanhood.

She is "a girl in her position"; "girls of that class" and "a girl of that sort". To Sybil, Arthur and Sheila, she is always a girl and never a young woman.

The only merit any of the characters concedes in Eva, or evaluates her by, is the fact that she was young and/or pretty. Gerald says she is "young, fresh and charming"; "young, pretty and warm-hearted". Arthur Birling remembers her as "country-bred"- like a horse or a sheep, perhaps?

The Birlings, and Gerald, use the language and euphemisms of prostitution when they refer to Eva.

Mrs Birling identifies her as "that sort" of girl, a girl in a particular position; Mr Birling talks of her "condition"; Eric says she was going to have a baby and Gerald uses the phrase "keep a girl".

The Palace Theatre bar is a favourite haunt of "women of the town" rather than prostitutes – the closest anyone comes to that word is Eric describing the women there as fat old tarts.

The Inspector, too, talks of "these young women who get into various kinds of trouble". He also speculates that "she enjoyed being among pretty clothes, I've no doubt" (whilst working at the department store). But to our modern minds, it remains sexist.

To our modern eyes, (we are, it must be remembered, living around 100 years after this play is set) this language is old-fashioned, anti-equality, unfair and sexist.

The inference in the play is that working-class girls can be sexualised and have no intrinsic intelligence, merit or value; older prostitutes are fat, hard-faced and doughy.

Gerald goes to the bar after a rather long dull day, and Eva has the misfortune of standing out, to him and then to Eric, because she is young and pretty with big eyes and soft brown hair.

Mr Birling regards his own daughter as a young unmarried girl, but as wholly respectable.

Sheila and her parents disagree at various points over whether Sheila, even at 24, is a child or a young woman (and Mrs Birling tries to excuse Eric's drunkenness on the grounds that he's only a boy even though he is in his early twenties).

We need to remember that 1912 pre-dated the time when women could take university degrees (1920) or vote (1928), and that Priestley is presenting us with realistic depictions of both class-based and gender-based attitudes towards women.

The First World War would make women more active economically and more autonomous generally; a process repeated and advanced by the Second World War.

Respectability and scandal

Arthur Birling is obsessed with the idea of his own social standing. That is why the idea of a knighthood appeals to him so much; it will make him more equal to the Croft family. Priestley sets his drama up with Birling expecting to be notified of his honour very soon- provided his family can stay out of trouble and out of the courts. Flagging this up during his conversation with Gerald near the start of the play is a sure sign that it will be put in doubt.

Gerald and Eric (and the appalling Alderman Meggarty) are drawn to the stalls bar at the Palace Theatre, which is "a favourite haunt of women of the town" i.e. prostitutes.

The Inspector asks Eric whether he was meeting Eva/Daisy by appointment – which would indicate a commercial sexual relationship rather than a personal one.

The Inspector excuses Gerald on the grounds that his relationship with her involved some real feeling; Sheila, too, makes some allowances for the fact that Gerald had felt sorry for her, and wanted to help her, but took advantage of her vulnerability and gratitude to keep her as his mistress.

Mrs Birling turns a blind eye to Eric's drinking, which Gerald and Sheila both know is problematic, while Mr Birling has failed to give Eric enough to do in the factory business, and taken too little interest in his hobbies. Their motto seems to be "see no evil, hear no evil". Mrs Birling tells Sheila not to resist Gerald's smooth claim to have been working hard when he failed to be attentive to her (a part- truth and a part- lie, because he was seeing Eva); there is an understanding that young men will indulge in sex with lower class women, and that it is acceptable provided no scandal attaches to it.

As Mr Birling says, an inquest into Eva's death, which named Eric as the father of her unborn child, would be highly embarrassing.

Even the King had been involved in a sexual scandal; as a young man, in 1870, he was alleged to have been one of several lovers of Harriet Mordaunt, whose husband, Sir Charles, sought a divorce because she told him he was not the father of her child.

This nod- and-a wink liberalism towards extra- marital sex is relevant to the characterisation of Gerald and Eric; it explains why Mr Birling thinks that Sheila does not need to break off her (socially desirable) engagement, while she is no longer prepared to accept the loose and imprecise personal morality of her parents' generation.

The Inspector says that he does not know where to draw the line between respectable citizens and criminals. He means that families like the Birlings and the Crofts may appear to the outside world to be solid and reliable citizens, but that, just beneath the surface, they exhibit the deadly sins of greed, lust, anger, pride and so on.

And now ... Mastering Essays

After reading this far, you should have a great deal to say about Priestley's aims, his message, and his skill in constructing his plot.

And yet.........you may still be feeling short of confidence, as you face the task of writing an essay under exam conditions. That's perfectly understandable, because nerves can play a part- and because you may not have written enough essays to feel that you have a strong method that will stand up to the stresses of a timed exam.

So here's what we're going to do in the final section of this guide.

- We'll look at two possible exam essay questions.
- We'll plan our answer.
- And we'll write our answer.

Always bear in mind that, depending on the exam you're taking, you'll have between 40 and 60 minutes for this- considerably less time than it takes to read either the play or this guide! So you need to work swiftly, but with care.

The more at home you are with the plot, the characters and the themes, the easier it becomes ... not least because you don't have to waste time struggling to recall what was the name of that son, (for example) and was it Mr B or Mr (Gerald) C who was the stupid one...

In my experience of studying exam questions from past papers, I have found that, in the questions that they set, *the examiners are trying to make it straightforward for you to show what you know.* They are not out to trick you!

Here's the first question that (in similar words) you could expect to get.

Essay 1

"Appearance and reality are so far apart in this play that it stops being believable". To what extent do you agree with this assessment of *An Inspector Calls* ?

Planning the answer

First, we need to gather together the material for our answer. It is the evidence from which we will construct our argument.

Note that we do not write our introduction until we have gathered our material, weighed up our evidence and worked out our argument.

Here's some material-

-The Birling family seems respectable (but it isn't)

-The Inspector seems real (but he isn't)

-Eva Smith seems to be real (but she could be an invention of the Inspector- or could she?)

-Eva Smith seems to be dead- then she doesn't- then she does (a suicide, but no body)

-The Birlings seem to take on board what the Inspector tells them, but then some of them back away from it

-Sheila seems happy, but she isn't

-The characters have secrets; what's real is not what's apparent

Now for the argument.

Does the fact that we're unsure about the facts get in the way of understanding the play?

If it does, then Priestley has failed; and the play has been very popular in theatres all over the world. But if the point is that some behaviours are like crimes (of conscience), even if they are not crimes in the legal sense, then Priestley is using the ambiguity to make the meaning of the play clear to us. He also gains by putting the audience through some of the same confusion the characters experience (apart from the Inspector).

Our plan needn't be more complicated than that, except that we will need to attach a relevant example or quotation to each point we make. Our conclusion comes from our argument, and our introduction just states our position; then we go straight to the evidence.

So here goes.

"An Inspector Calls" depends for its dramatic effect on the idea that we can excuse our own bad behaviour to ourselves, but that there is a moral standard which we should judge ourselves by. The play exposes its characters- under examination by the Inspector- to the implications and consequences of their actions, and it joins its audience with those characters in inviting us to learn from the things we have done in the past which make us feel "ashamed", as Sheila puts it.

Rather than confusing us, the unreality is part of Priestley's method; whether Eva/Daisy is dead or not, what was done to her was real. We side with Sheila (and Eric), who have learned to behave differently, and, like the Inspector, we "lose all patience" with Arthur and Sybil Birling and Gerald Croft, who regard the investigation as nothing more serious than a frightening hoax.

In the opening scene, Gerald tells Mr Birling that his family seems well-behaved, and Mr Birling says "we think we are".

Later in Act One, Gerald protests to the Inspector that "we're respectable citizens and not criminals", only to be told that "there isn't as much difference as you think". Sheila and her mother abuse their power, so that Eva is sacked from Milwards and receives no help from the Women's Charity. Mr Birling sacked Eva for being a troublemaker; he too failed to consider what might become of her. Gerald and Eric both used Eva/Daisy for their sexual gratification.

Gerald, by today's standards, was unfaithful to his intended fiancée, and Eric stole from his father. Mrs Birling did not murder her unborn grandchild in the literal sense; but she cannot escape responsibility for what she did wrong.

The second half of the play hinges on the growing suspicion that the Inspector is not a real police officer; what are the implications of that? Sheila is the first to suggest that he may not be "real", but that does not make him a "fake". If he were an orthodox policeman, the Inspector's investigation would peter out, because there is no literal crime to prosecute.

The opinions he expresses (on behalf of the "millions of John Smiths and Eva Smiths") and the warning in his final speech of the cataclysm which will follow if we neglect the concept of "community" are not what a policeman would say; he does ask the extensive questions we would expect, as he interrogates the characters (they cannot be said to be "suspects").

When he says that he is "losing all patience with you people", we empathise with him- we are convinced enough of his substance, though he is an inspector of conscience- a special and unusual aspect of crime. The nature of his investigation means that he cannot and should not be too like someone we recognise as a naturalistic police officer. The difference is important.

Arthur Birling and Gerald Croft seize on Sheila's doubts, to check that there is no Inspector Goole in the local force, and that no girl has died in hospital of drinking disinfectant. They grasp at this like drowning men at a straw, because they think it lets them off the hook. They then convince themselves that the Inspector's use of the photograph supports the theory that there is no one girl. Both Sheila, and we, the audience, find this incredible and irrelevant.

The Eva Smith whom Birling and Sheila drove out of her jobs, and who called herself Mrs Birling in front of the charity committee, is the same girl- the girl whose prettiness and liveliness makes her an easy target, and who never seeks revenge or justice when she is ill-treated. The change of name- from Eva, to Daisy Renton- is convincing, and her fall into prostitution and misery is a single, continuous arc.

Because the wrongs done to Eva are real enough, it does not matter that there has been no suicide in Brumley for months. The Inspector insists, throughout, on her physical pain- to shock Sheila and the others, so that they are more inclined to answer his questions honestly- so that it surprises us that there is no suicide. But this is another dramatic thrust, because it makes possible the crushing phone call which brings the final curtain down. The generation gap, and the gulf between the baggage of the old individualism and the new sense of community, is clearer because, as Eric and Sheila realise, it does not matter whether there has been a death- if there has not, there easily could have been.

Arthur and Sybil Birling (and Gerald) seem to be humbled by what the Inspector says and does- but only while he is in their house. They resist and complain about his manner and what he says- as though he is not deferential enough to his social superiors. They see the fact that he is more than/not quite human as discrediting his message.

The friction between the Birling parents and their children dramatises and symbolises the friction between the pre-War and post-War insights and values.

Sheila appears at first to be committed to marrying Gerald, but she is uneasy about his unexplained lack of interest in her the previous summer- when he was keeping a girl. Although her parents see Gerald's behaviour as acceptable, Sheila says they are now different people; having rejected the ring, she will not take it back, because Gerald needs to prove his integrity and prove to her that he can be caring and honest. It could happen; it may not.

Sheila rewrites the code by which she will marry and live, and she loosens the straitjacket of feminine submissiveness and passivity. She deals with the consequences of Gerald's deceit, where her parents want to ignore it; in doing so, she eliminates the gap between reality and appearance, and becomes sadder but wiser.

Mr Birling's secret knighthood and his fear of scandal, Gerald's secret liaison and his vanity, Sheila's secret viciousness, Eric's secret unborn child and his (not so secret) drinking, Mrs Birling's secret class snobbishness (she helps the poor with her charity, yet despises them), the Birlings' inadequacies as parents, and Eva's secret nobility all emerge into the open under the harshly lit gaze of the Inspector- who has known all of the truth from the start, but reveals it to the characters themselves and to the audience.

The plot of the play takes place over a single evening- although the action will be repeated after the audience has left the theatre(!). Priestley stretches the boundaries between fact and fiction, the real and the unreal, in order to highlight the moral dimension of our everyday actions. The convention of the police "whodunit" heightens the drama, even though there is no murder.

The reality of what lies under the surface of a "well-behaved" middle class household is exposed; and we see the damage done by arrogance, selfishness and the misuse of power. Dramatising morality is difficult to do. Priestley manages it by making the unreal real and the real unreal.

Essay 2

How does Priestley make the Inspector such a memorable and important figure in the play?

The dramatist has choices to make about characterisation, language and stage directions- our answer needs to cover all three.

Material

Characterisation of the Inspector- his behaviour/focus/insistence /bluntness. Symbolism. Realistic/unrealistic elements. Unconventionality. His name.

Language of the Inspector- threatening, prophetic, biblical, moralistic.

Stage directions about the Inspector- when he first appears, and to describe how he speaks.

His role in the drama: central, but absent towards the end.

(Note. In this question, the word "how" is the key- it requires us to explain Priestley's methods, not just state facts.)

Answer

The Inspector is a man in his fifties who wears a business suit and has a particular way of speaking and looking at people. His methods are autocratic and slightly odd, but he is so dominant that the characters he is "inspecting"- whom he has taken by surprise- tend to go along with him ("I'm easy with you if you're easy with me").

His behaviour is very focused- on exposing the truth (which he already knows), or rather exposing the characters' secrets and sins. He refuses to be patronised, bribed, threatened, or taken aside into a corner; he does not want to play golf, and he can always be relied on to do his "duty".

He tells Gerald that he finds it hard to draw the line between criminals and the law-abiding, and he says that enquiries of this sort (the investigation of crimes against morality and community) are left to him. He is sharp with Arthur and Sybil Birling, but much less aggressive towards Sheila, Eric and Gerald, who are readier to admit their own faults. He is not interested in tensions within the Birling household; he tells them they will have plenty of time to adjust their relationships later.

The combination of control, refusing digressions, and his insistence that time is short, as we move towards the apparent climax of the action, puts the Inspector "in charge". He is on stage almost continuously- he only leaves for a very short scene at the very end of Act One between Sheila and Gerald. But the play starts and ends without him; it still has 20% of its length to run after he leaves in Act Three. He is like an earthquake which leaves aftershocks. After he has exposed the individual and collective guilt of the Birlings and Gerald, we do see them "adjusting", with interesting consequences, which include replaying the whole drama to see if the lessons can be learnt second time around.

The Inspector's function is not just dramatic. He is symbolic, too. In Greek drama, the "chorus" would intervene to tell the audience the truth and give moral guidance. The Inspector does this, for example when he says it would do us all good to try to "put ourselves in the place of "Eva Smith and those used as "cheap labour". He criticises Arthur Birling's refusal to give a pay rise; he tells Mrs Birling she has done "something terribly wrong".

He excuses Gerald because he made Eva "happy for a while". He therefore sees merit in unconventional relationships, as well as advocating workers' rights ("it's better to ask for the earth than to take it"). He is interested in whether Gerald was in love with Eva, and he tells Mrs Birling that "You've had children. You must have known what she was feeling". He condemns Eric for treating Eva/Daisy "as if she was an animal, a thing, not a person".

He approves of feeling, and disapproves of insensitivity- because the sense of responsibility to other people, of caring for the less fortunate and distressed, depends on the capacity to feel, which Sheila and Eric have, and their parents and the Croft family do not. The Inspector himself stands outside society- we know nothing about him, except that he is not part of the local police force. He appears at the moment when Arthur Birling is at his most pompous and selfish, preaching the doctrine of self-sufficiency. It seems that, rather like a crime-fighting superhero, he will appear, to confront and defeat the forces of immorality.

His name- Goole- is a pun on "ghoul"; he is the ghost of a guilty conscience, and his behaviour is slightly robotic, as though he does indeed inhabit a parallel world. He lacks humour and patience, but uses irony, sarcasm and pathos (in his repeated descriptions of how Eva died). He does not make small talk.

His values and his belief (in community and social responsibility) set him apart from the other characters. So does his language. The social message is compassionate and Christian; in his final speech, he borrows the mystical language of the Communion service ("we are members of one body"). His last words ("fire and blood and anguish") are like a prophecy from the Old Testament. Where the other characters talk in terms of manners, he talks only of morals (responsibility and guilt, which- again, like the church Communion - must be "shared").

He finds that redemption, though, is likelier for "the young ones" because "they're more impressionable". He wants to see an inclusive society, but it does not have to include those like the Birling parents who hate the idea of being "mixed up.......like bees in a hive". He accuses Mrs Birling of "not telling me the truth" and tells Mr Birling not to "stammer and yammer at me again"; he is blunt to the point of rudeness where necessary.

He sums up the case, and passes his final verdicts on each of the suspects, as though he is judge and jury, not an investigating police officer. There is no doubting his moral authority; nor that he is the mouthpiece for the social message Priestley wants the play to convey.

The stage directions bear this out. The actor must give "an impression of massiveness, solidity and purposefulness". This lack of interest in politeness or interpersonal skills elevates and narrows the range of the character, to establish his authority and difference.

Adverbs pepper the stage directions, to show how the Inspector uses his voice- coolly, gravely, dryly, slowly, impressively, massively, cutting in, sternly, with authority, sharply, severely, grimly, masterfully; like a judge, or perhaps like God! This is a serious man, on a serious mission, and he will not be deflected from it.

The Inspector, then, is rather an extra-terrestrial figure; judgmental, utterly clear and focused, detached from any personal involvement with those whose guilt he brings to the surface. He is convincing enough as a police officer to use conventional police techniques of questioning; but his purpose is to preach a gospel and to pass lasting moral judgments. In giving him the language of morality and of the Christian church, Priestley makes him unique in the canon of detectives.

Showing off a great essay technique- some valuable tips

Excluding Edna, but including Eva/Daisy, there are only six characters in the play; and Eva does not have a speaking part!! Nor is she on stage, although her photograph is. So there is no excuse for not knowing what each character says, how they behave, what their faults are, and what (if any) their journey is.

The themes of the play are very clear too. After reading this guide, you should be well informed about the mood of 1945 and the years after it; the reasons why the welfare state in Britain came to be set up as the predecessor of the one we have today; and why Priestley chose 1912 as the world of his drama.

Be clear too about what Priestley has to say about personal responsibility, civic society, welfare, the family, the rights of employees, social hierarchies, the place of men and women. (For a recap, turn back to page 11).

Before you take your exam, please spend some time thinking about the play *as a drama.* You don't have to see it in the theatre; picture what you read as a stage production as you read it. What surprises and unsettles you? Does the Inspector surprise and shock you? Does the sudden ending?

Try to put yourself in the position of each of the characters in turn, and then read their scenes where the Inspector interrogates them. How would you feel, knowing the guilty secrets each of them has? Then imagine you are the Inspector. How frustrating are these people?

If you can rope someone in to revise with you, why not read the play out loud together – take it in turns to be the inspector so that you can appreciate how it feels to be grilled as well as being the interrogator.

Work out what is in the play to make it more dramatic.

List and consider those things.

- a ringing telephone
- a photograph
- the Inspector's insistence on talking to one person at a time
- the use of dramatic irony and of foreshadowing (Eric's drinking, Sheila's anger, Gerald's neglect).
- the moment where Eric accuses his mother of killing her own grandchild (see how this is tragic and dramatic at the same time.)

Look at the odd moments of humour, and how few of them there are, because this is a serious play.

And think about how Priestley manages to make his characters seem real, three-dimensional.

We may not like them, but they have depth and they seem authentic. How has he done that?

Whatever your exam board is, look, on its website, not just at questions on past papers, but at the mark schemes and the examiners' reports. Ask your English teacher to demystify the mark scheme and give you some tips.

And a pitfall to avoid

Don't fall into the trap of having a list of quotations you're determined to force into any essay. If you know the play- which you surely must by now!!- suitable short references will pop into your head (a one or two word quotation often works well for this play).

Your number one focus is on answering the question in front of you.

Your number two focus is on answering the question.

So is focus number 3.

Answering the question means taking it apart and highlighting the key words (often that little word "how"); making a proper plan, which organises your material, gives you an argument and leads you to a clear and convincing conclusion; writing your essay from the plan; and stopping when you get to the end.

A proper plan means an essay that needs nothing added after its conclusion.

GCSE Exam Markers are always interested in your personal response (provided it's sensible, and explained) so don't be afraid to analyse, where you feel an emotional reaction to a line or scene. Distress, unease, empathy, frustration, pity- these are all part of our response to events and flashpoints in the drama, and they're a good clue to where our sympathies are intended to lie.

Please, please resist the temptation to start writing your essay straight away, even if many of those around you in the exam room do just that.

The exam allows you time to plan, and it is almost impossible to get a really good mark without a really good plan.

The test in the exam, then, is to choose relevant material, put it into an effective structure, and use your points to construct an argument, which you support by reference to the text, but not by copying out long quotations.

You should develop each of your points in one paragraph.

- Try to use fairly short sentences.
- When you have finished one point, go on to the next one.
- In your summary/concluding paragraph, you can say which point is the most important, and why.

Raise your grade tip:

Before you start writing your answer, put the points in your plan in order of importance. Write about them in order of importance, with the most important ones first.

That way, if you run out of time for that question, you'll only have left out your least important material.

Don't try to write too much, but *check-constantly-that what you are writing is actually answering the question in front of you.* If it isn't- leave it out.

Especially if you are taking your GCSE this summer, I wish you every success.

Gavin Smithers is a private tutor, covering Broadway, Chipping Campden and the North

Cotswolds. He has an English degree from Oxford University, and a passion for helping others to discover the joy and satisfaction of great literature.

Gavin's Guides are short books packed with insight. Their key aim is to help you raise your grade!

The series, which now includes analyses of John Steinbeck's Of Mice and Men and Charles Dickens's Great Expectations, is available in e-book and paperback. Details and reviews of the series are on Gavin Smithers' Amazon page.

And finally.........if there's anything you're still not sure about, and if your teacher can't help, contact the author- grnsmithers@hotmail.co.uk

12397635R00073

Printed in Great Britain
by Amazon.co.uk, Ltd.,
Marston Gate.